BOY ~~DON'T~~ DO CRY

Compiled and Published by
Michelle Catanach

uncagedonline

'Raising boys to hide their feelings increases their sense of overwhelming loneliness. Emotions are gender-free. Everyone feels every feeling. It's part of being human.'

Jane Evans
Internationally Renowned Childhood Trauma,
Parenting & Anxiety Expert
(www.thejaneevans.com)

All royalties from the sale of this book are to be shared equally between the following two charities:

Positive Signs aims to positively affect people's moods, outlooks and lives through meaningful creative interventions.

Depression is the leading cause of disability worldwide. In Australia, it's estimated that 45 per cent of people will experience a mental health condition in their lifetime. Add to this a high-rotation news cycle filled with endless images of fear and destruction, and advertising that tells us we're never quite good enough. It can all become overwhelming - and sometimes tragically so.

We know we can't solve every problem for everyone - but we believe we can help some people, sometimes. If we can replace a negative message with a positive one, or take a cold blank space and turn it into somewhere warm and supportive, that's a good start. Be it a wall, postcard, billboard, or social media post, every Positive Sign we create has the potential to improve the happiness in someone's life.

To learn more about Positive Signs visit:
www.positivesigns.net.au

Campaign Against Living Miserably (CALM)

The Campaign Against Living Miserably (CALM) is an award-winning charity dedicated to preventing male suicide, the single biggest killer of men under the age of 45 in the UK. In 2015, 75% of all UK suicides were male.

Our work includes:

❖ **Offering support** to men in the UK, of any age, who are down or in crisis via our helpline, webchat and website

❖ **Challenging a culture** that prevents men seeking help when they need it, through CALMzine and campaigns such as #ManDictionary and #BiggerIssues

❖ **Pushing for changes in policy and practice** so that suicide is better prevented, via partnerships such as The Alliance of Suicide Prevention Charities (TASC), the National Suicide Prevention Alliance (NSPA)

❖ **Supporting those bereaved by suicide**, through the Support After Suicide Partnership (SASP), hosted by CALM, which aims to ensure that everyone bereaved or affected by suicide is offered and receives timely and appropriate support.

CALM is a registered charity No. 1110621 and SCO44347. To find out more about CALM visit: **www.thecalmzone.net**

Foreword
By Terry Earthwind Nicholls

'We are born with an already established personality. As we age, we become witness to various stimuli that change the way we look at the world and how we will act and react in it'. ~ Terry Earthwind Nichols

I was a child of the 50's and 60's. Although peace and love were all over radio and television, the rough and tough mining town I lived in was not about peace and love, but rather who was the toughest. Sound familiar?

The brutality of growing up as a boy is not unique to mining towns in the US Rocky Mountains, ghettos of East Los Angeles or even the barrios of Barcelona, Spain. The 'toughest' one rules. Organised gangs are the worst for they demand loyalty and obedience. Does this make sense? Let's expand on this thought some more.

Where there is high poverty, there is high brutality, usually as an outlet for frustration. We are not born as mean people. We are taught to be mean and to keep our wits about us for protection, much the same as was necessary thousands of years ago. Back in the early times, brutality was used to maintain the hierarchy of the community similar to dog packs. The biggest and strongest was alpha and so on down the pecking order to the workers or lesser members, who were weak but used their brains to survive.

Over the millennia, the leaders of communities figured out that their bloodline produced more consistent leaders. They started having their children reproduce with other leaders' off-spring to keep a stronger bloodline going. This theory was passed down and how modern society began. Now back to brutality.

Brutality has always been used to control the masses, causing followers to fear their leader. Fear also became respect for what those leaders had accomplished and acquired for the community. The more horrible the brutality, the more control the leaders had over the community. History has shown us a lot of examples of those horrors.

Let's talk about kids growing up in our general society today, which perpetuates violence in every facet of their daily life from video games to movies to television to newspapers. Violence sells because even in these days of living well, compared to just one hundred years ago, we are not satisfied with what we have. Our mentality is an, 'I want what they have' mentality. Media helps us to think that way too on a daily basis.

So, what did brutality look like in my little town in the mountains? Mining towns are high violence, low pay, slave mentality communities. Just ask a coal miner. For the mines to get plenty of labour at low wages, they must hire people with little or no education so they can manipulate them into the slavery they are entering. The fact that these people are desperate sets the stage for economic slavery. Our teachers and principals had to be pro-mine and not pro-people. Otherwise they were fired and replaced quickly.

Friday night was 'fight night' where I lived, including my parents who drank too much, partied too hard, and ended Friday nights with a fight at home. Every week was the same. My parents would hire a sitter for my older brother and me. She always had to be home by eleven o'clock. I was a light sleeper if I slept at all. Once she left, I was all alone. At least that is how it felt. Home alone on fight night, while my brother slept peacefully in his bed, until the fight bell rang around one o'clock.

Ding! Mom and Dad were home, and so it began with, 'Terry go to bed,' coming from one of them. The screaming would start followed with slamming cabinet doors and broken dishes – then the 'slap' sound. I never did figure out who slapped who. Within minutes all were in bed and silence came over the house for the rest of the night.

Silence isn't as peaceful as one would imagine, for in the silence the 'demons' come out and play with your head and make you afraid to close your eyes. I equated sleep with violence – violence was brutal and expected where I lived. It's what I knew; I thought it was normal.

My earliest memory of violence in school was in third grade when two kids started to fight over a candy bar. They were older boys of around ten years and were known to fight a lot at school. This time they brutally beat on each other until two teachers and the principle broke them up. They were dragged away to the 'dungeon', the principal's office, where they were both spanked with a huge wooden paddle.

Each boy knew that they could not lose the fight because they would be beaten up by their father when they got home, for losing, rather than for fighting. This 'must-win' mentality made a tussle into a fight to the death if necessary, even for a candy bar. My first fight was in the fifth grade with my best friend at the time, and over a girl. Why are men always fighting over women? Well, she loved it, and even though I was winning and had given my friend a black eye, I stopped and walked away without even looking at the girl. I felt saddened that I had just lost my best friend over a girl I didn't even want.

Middle school was pretty tame compared to high school. I got into a scrape once and saw very quickly that I was set up to see how tough I was, by the bullies in the school. I laughed at my opponent and walked away. The bullies tried a few times to get me to fight one of their underlings. They failed to entice me every time because I saw right through their schemes. Interesting to note that none of the bullies ever bothered me directly. I found out later in life that they had respected me, even though I didn't fight. I was one of the lucky ones. Other boys in my schools were not so lucky and were beaten up pretty regularly. They were victims ripe for the picking and probably continued through life as victims.

In my work, my clients have been life-long victims of one sort or another: PTSD, Suicide Ideation, and self-sabotage. They have dealt with victimisation of various types, such as weight issues, relationship issues, and more. All of them have had one thing in common—an extremely emotional event that occurred in early childhood. It's a memory that they can't even remember until they go through a process that I developed as a way to deal with my own self-sabotaging behaviour.

As stated in many of the stories in this book, I have found that most men walk through a 'wasteland of terror'. A fear that haunts them day and night to a point they can't even function anymore.

To survive in this world, we begin to protect ourselves in various ways, and one, in particular, is called 'masking'. Here in the US, we wear masks and make-up for a holiday called Halloween. In general, when we wear a false cover, something happens inside of us. We are the hero. Something else happens even more powerful – we are a hero, *and* we are 'protected' from the world that hurts us all of the time!

We start by acting like the hero, the mask we wore for Halloween, for one more day, two more days, three more days and so on to protect ourselves. When we are a hero, we are okay inside, and it feels good. Taking this another step further, we also notice when people like us. We perform in certain ways, such as being funny or perhaps overly helpful and they love us for it. All of a sudden, an 'aha' moment occurs, and we start to become that person over and over. Why? For protection and love!

Many of us adopt many different masks and use them to fit various situations. Perhaps we use one for attracting the attention of a girl. Perhaps we use another to keep the bullies away.

Anyone who presents to us as dangerous is a bully. An arrogant boss, a teacher, priest, father, someone who physically wants to hurt or rob us. All of these threats are real to us and feel dangerous! Bullies vary in intensity, hence the assumed need for various masks. There is another way to protect ourselves, and that is by being a 'Social Chameleon'.

A chameleon is a lizard that can change its physical appearance to reflect its surroundings. I am a chameleon and a very accomplished one because I didn't fight the bullies. I blended in with them so they couldn't see me and, therefore, couldn't fight me. Today I can easily walk into a crowd of people and disappear – protection!

We, as boys becoming men, want to love and be loved for being a 'manly man' like 007 or Beckham. When we find that we cannot, something horrible happens inside of us – 'man shame'.

Let's talk about 'man shame', which can be deadly. First and foremost, it comes with suicide ideation. Thinking about what a loser we are for not being smart, handsome, and rich. To some of you reading this, you may be thinking, *really? 'Man shame' is connected to suicide'?* YES, even suicide! It's important to realise that suicide doesn't stop with the person who ends their own life. It perpetuates throughout families, increasing the chance that someone else in the family will end their life as well. Children who have lost a parent to suicide have a 2 in 5 chance that they too will commit suicide.

'Man shame' will come at you over and over until it is neutralised. So how is this accomplished? The process I created has proven to be a great and consistent non-behavioural health tool. I call it The CR Process©. It's a very specific question and answer sequence to help the client find, identify, and neutralise an amnesic memory found in early childhood. Amnesia is a protection system that keeps us from remembering events with high emotional value.

When a severe emotional event occurs to a child who can't even talk yet, two things happen. 1) The child can't tell anyone what just happened and 2) they don't know what just happened to them – only that it was bad and probably hurt.

My research findings have revealed that 80% of the time something sexual happened, meaning anything from inappropriate touch to full sexual intercourse of an adult with a child.

Whereas for the other 20%, an adult said something 'stupid' or inappropriate to a child and the child reacted with high emotion that the adult did not observe. One of two things have happened here: 1) the adult didn't know they caused damage or 2) they had no remorse and did nothing to fix the damage before it became amnesic in its makeup.

I learned to cry in secret as a small child. I used to hear, 'Big boys don't cry,' or 'Stop crying or I'll give something to cry about'. That was my life growing up. As an adult, I found that I could cry only during the late-night hours in bed, while my former wife was asleep. The crying was very quiet and always followed by 'man shame'.

I am now a man who is present with himself and with others! These days, I cry wherever I damn well please. I trust that this writing will start you on your way to being yourself too. You see? *Boys DO Cry!*

I am very honoured to have been chosen to write the foreword for this very moving anthology by Michelle Catanach. Thank you very much, Michelle!

Best regards, Terry Earthwind Nichols.

Repetitive Behavior Cellular Regression™ *(RBCR) or The CR Process©, as stated above, is based on a non-linear Q & A sequencing model that uses alternative neuropathways to help clients find, identify, and neutralise an amnesic event that controls their repetitive thoughts/behaviours and can produce a life of suffering. This process is accomplished online using an audio/visual platform where the practitioner can observe the client as they go through the session, which usually lasts between 2 and 3 hours. There are follow-up calls and client work after the session. I have provided links below so you can contact me personally, as well as find more information, including videos, about The CR Process.*

Website:

Evolutionary Healer LLC:
www.EvolutionaryHealer.com

White Paper on Repetitive Behavior Cellular
Regression™: www.evolutionaryhealer.com/white-paper-on-repetitive-behavior

YouTube:

EvolutionaryHealer:
www.youtube.com/channel/UCpMe7QbrODv8shbXPRR5
EBw

Connect with Terry:

Email: terry@evolutionaryhealer.com
Telephone: +1 (828) 676-2535
Facebook: Terry Nichols
Twitter: @earthwindhealer
LinkedIn: Terry Earthwind Nichols

A Message from Michelle Catanach

The idea for this book came to me as I was about to publish women's anthology *Uncaged: The Rise of the Badass* post #metoo. I was thinking about my then three-year-old son and wondering about the type of man he would grow up to be. I thought about my six-year-old daughter, contemplating how effective it would be raising a girl with a voice and clear boundaries if these couldn't protect her from the actions of those around her.

Growing up I felt more connected to boys and men than I did girls and women; misogyny lives within us all, women too. Yet I couldn't help observing the extent to which boys are also the victim of a deeply wounded, abusive culture.

Love, compassion and empathy are innate; our natural birth state. I've witnessed the purest levels of empathy in my son and daughter when they were 18 months and nine months old respectively. Yet for so many boys their natural state of being is shamed out of them to fit social and cultural masculine ideology. Stereotypes and rules are forced upon them. We seek evidence to support and justify 'natural' male behaviour – boys will be boys, after all - rather than seeing the truth of what much of it is: learned.

More people are waking up to the impact of childhood

trauma and emotional suppression on mental health later on in life, and more needs to be done. By following the narrative that boys should think, feel and behave a certain way, by shaming them for crying and expressing any emotion other than anger or joy, is denying them their humanity. It's denying them the opportunity to grow into healthy, functioning adults. Boys are human, in the same way that girls are. And all emotions are *human* emotions; there is no gender bias.

When it comes to raising our sons, the harsh reality is this: we're letting our boys down.

I have been deeply moved by the chapters in this book and touched by the courage and willingness of the co-authors to express themselves in ways that go against cultural norms. If we are to shift the trajectory of humanity and create a more peaceful, less harmful world for our children, we each need to look inside ourselves and face our deepest, darkest, innermost wounds, and be radically honest about how we have perpetuated and enabled a culture that glorifies destruction and violence.

My hope is that this book will elicit some much needed conversations with our partners, friends, colleagues and children and open our hearts to a better, kinder, more loving and compassionate way of being; the way we always were. Let's support each other. Let's nurture our boys for the tender souls that they are. Let's lift the veil, drop the masks, and step into a more authentic way of being that creates acceptance, of ourselves and others.

Michelle xo

www.michellecatanach.co.uk
www.uncaged.online

Michelle Catanach – Author, Artist & Creative Coach - is on a mission to end violence against women and children. She helps people of all ages be more of who they already are using the power of art and writing as tools for healing, activism and authentic self-expression. She is also the founder of Uncaged Online, a self-publishing platform to help emerging thought leaders and paradigm shifters change the world with their words.

To our rising boys: stay true to your tender heart.

Contents

Introduction

Mental health problems (e.g. depression, anxiety and drug use) are one of the main causes of the overall disease burden in the world. In the UK, 84 men commit suicide every week, rising to 123 per day in the US. In Australia, men are three times more likely to commit suicide than women, and it is estimated that there are approximately 65,300 suicide attempts each year.

As much as women have been disfigured by the patriarchy, men have too.

From birth boys are given a very disempowering view of what it means to be a *real* man, told to 'man up', that 'boys don't cry', their tenderness and empathy shamed out of them and replaced with a tough, armoured exterior.

They learn that women are objects, machismo and misogyny becoming a badge of honour in a world that otherwise leaves them feeling lost, disconnected and unsure of who they're meant to be. They learn to fight for survival, that success and power are everything, and without them, they're nothing.

As a result, men have suffered, suppressing their emotions and only learning unhealthy expressions of anger, often manifesting as addiction and violence towards other men, women and – ultimately – themselves.

In *Boys Do Cry*, 12 men bare their souls, expose their wounds, and share their breakdown-breakthrough moments to change the narrative around masculinity and inspire men of all ages to step into the man they deeply desire to be.

Clear your mind, open your heart, and get ready to go on a journey of truth and vulnerability as we redefine what it means to be a man.

Removing the Masks
By Spencer Jacobs

'Fear is present when we forget that we are a part of God's divine design. Learning to experience authentic love means abandoning ego's insistence that you have much to fear and that you are in an unfriendly world. You can make the decision to be free from fear and doubt and return to the brilliant light of love that is always with you.' ~ Wayne Dyer

My name is Spencer Jacobs, and I am 50 years of age. I strive daily to interact with the rest of humanity with love and compassion. But I have a problem. A problem carried in the collective pain-body of humankind, particularly men.

Anger.

I have a problem with anger and authentic expression. I have a problem with vulnerability. I have a problem with people.

I used to believe that this would never change but I was wrong. Over the past 15 years, life has changed for the better. I still fail, but I never give up trying. I am learning to think with my heart more and aim to be a better human every day.

In the last six years, I have finally begun to understand my place and purpose as a man in this world, and in the last year, I have made incredible strides in the way I interact with my fellow man. I try to live each day as a man of integrity and authenticity, but I walked in the dark about what that meant for 30 years.

Now don't get me wrong, there are a few things I'd like to clarify before we dive into my story.

Firstly, I take full responsibility for my life and for the man I used to be. While the pervading culture around me hid the true nature of masculinity and paraded falsehoods at every turn, it was I who bought into every myth and every mask. Using bravado to disguise my constant fear. Using banter and insults to deflect vulnerability. Using sexual fantasy and sexual conquests to distract me from my self-loathing. Treating those around me who showed any glimpse of vulnerability with contempt. I did all that. Nobody made me be that way. I and I alone am responsible for my actions.

Secondly, my upbringing was fairly typical for a man of my era. My perception of what was required to be a man was based on studying men around me. I thought men were much the same and I was the odd one out. I know now that everyone is unique on the inside. There may be fundamental similarities in the human experience, but laid over that simple canvas is an infinite number of beautiful patterns of human expression, all of them right and true. We are all of us beautiful and unique, *all of us* God's children.

Thirdly, I want to state that I am a work in progress. I have not conquered anger, and I certainly do not always express myself authentically. I am human and afflicted with all of the same triggers and patterns as any other human being. I would say however that they no longer conflict me; we coexist. It's all part of the healing.

You may see things in my story that you recognise. If you too want to change the way you are in this world, then take what you will from these pages. I am on a journey. We all are. And I hope my story gets you a little closer to what you're searching for.

My Earliest Memory

My earliest memory is of summer 1977. The memory is so vivid that even now I can see, smell and taste the past as if it is unfolding right in front of me.

I am crying behind the bar of my father's pub in Wales. This is my home. It is four thirty on a Friday afternoon. The pub is closed. I am 10 years old, and the blood is pouring from my nose from a boxing match I had just had with my best friend at the time. My father had allowed us to fight with gloves under his supervision, a very typical East end past time and one that was very popular after the release of *Rocky*.

My fight had been short and brutal. It was a painful and humiliating introduction into the art of violence. As we trudged back indoors, I felt so ashamed at my performance that the tears began to roll down my cheeks. My father turned to tell me something and, seeing the sadness and shame pouring out of me, said what a lot of fathers might have said in 1977.

'Stop crying boy. Dry your eyes. You got a proper pasting there because you dropped your guard. Never drop your guard. Dry your fucking eyes and get everyone some cokes.'

For a very long time afterwards, the shame of this rebuke ignited the first spark of anger within me when confrontation seemed imminent. It stoked 20 years of confrontation with the world. As I've begun to heal my pain more recently and my heart has begun to open, I've come to realise that my father did not know any better. I believe that he is as much the product of *his* past as I am of mine.

My father grew up in the East end of London after the war. Aged 12 he lost his father. He survived abject poverty, social stigma, abuse and bullying at the hands of other children to become a volatile, brooding young man who left his childhood behind, yet never shrugged off his past. I believe that my father's childhood left him scarred. The loss of his father and the fear and anger he felt turned him into a distant, verbally abusive man incapable of empathy. I think life hardened him and as a consequence of his experiences, he loathed vulnerability, in himself and others. He was prone to bouts of rage.

I have shed many tears over the years thinking about that little boy with no dad. I know that inside of him is a beautiful soul and a wise mind. He is a bright star, and I hope one day that he shines his true light and shows the world what he is capable of.

I knew none of this on that summer afternoon. His look of disgust when he saw my tears caused feelings of shame to explode to the surface wrapping its hands around my neck for the first time. As I gathered the bottles of coke, flipping the tops and hearing the fizz of air escape from each bottle, I wished I was someone else. Someone hard. Someone handy. Someone who didn't feel like this. I hated those tears. I hated that I couldn't fight, hated that my dad thought I was a crybaby. I hated him and everyone else. Most of all I hated myself, and at that moment the flower of anger and aggression first budded inside me. I put the bottles of coke down, and I dried my fucking eyes.

I heard the voice inside me.

'Stop crying, stop feeling this way. Stop acting like a girl. Stop!'

This voice would later drive me to extreme anger and abusive communication with others in later life.

When the Rot Sets In

I spent much of my teenage years and early manhood in a state of low-level anxiety and self-loathing. A bullying family member diminished my confidence, and I considered myself a bit of a coward with average intelligence. As puberty loomed, I considered myself a freak. If people saw me for who I was, they would laugh and sneer. I wanted to fit in. I wanted to be ok.

I hatched a plan when I was 13 years old. I thought that if I simply acted like the older boys I saw around me, then people would be fooled into thinking I was normal. I was good at mimicking so I figured that pretending to be strong and tough would be easy. I knew I couldn't ever become a strong man, but I could pretend. I could mask who I really was. I could hide my fear, hide my shame and hide my loneliness.

I began to think of my appearance like a mask. If I was scared, then I would act angry. If I was lonely, then I would act cold, and if I was sad, I would act excited and animated.

Like any good mimic, I studied my subjects well. Some men were hard, cold, and didn't talk much. Others were charming and predatory. All were - as far as I could tell - unfeeling, relentless automatons, smelling weakness and punishing softness through verbal or physical violence. During the 1980s in Wales, there were plenty of examples like these to study. I watched men's faces and listened to their language. I studied their gait, their image. I watched them laugh and shout, banter and fight. I soon realised that I needed more men to study, so music and film became my next teachers.

My first film hero was James Bond, my second Tony Montana. Violence and sexual conquest hand in hand. I studied the rogues, the gangsters, and the Casanovas. My music taste further enforced my warped worldview of masculinity.

As a small boy, I had loved the freedom and joy of disco. After my boxing match beating, I chose a darker form more fitting of my view of the world. Where I grew up, everyone listened to heavy metal, and I was no different. The tone of the genre perfectly matched my new dark, brooding view of life. This fusion of hard-edged riffs and doom-laden lyrics was the soundtrack to my world as a teenager. In 1983 I discovered hip-hop and my love affair with toxic masculinity began in earnest.

Aged 14 I believed all *real* men drank too much alcohol, took drugs, partied all night and slept with as many girls as they could. On top of this bonfire of vanities, I poured over the petrol of pornography. From this toxic brew, I fashioned my masks of manhood and soon began to rely on these masks to get me through most days. Masks are such lovely, dreadful things. They don't take much energy to maintain, and you feel safe behind them. Only at night, alone in my room, would I finally remove them. There I would stand and stare in the mirror, telling myself everything was going to be ok. I believed that once I left the small village where I grew up, I could leave my fear and my masks behind.

Some of these masks are still with me today.

My First Glimpse of Heaven

In August 1987, I went to university in London. I wanted to escape from my small life and go back to the city of my birth. I desperately wanted to be a London boy, but quickly realised that it would never be my home. I was never going to fit in. All the attitude but none of the wisdom. Lacking the understanding and lacking the accent. Not accepted. Not authentic. Trying too hard to be a wide boy. Another mask. Another lie.

Once again all of my fears around my perceived inadequacies were alive within me. I had fled, only for the fear and self-loathing I thought I'd escaped, to track me down. I clutched my masks tightly through that first term at university hoping that something or someone would come along and save me from myself

In January 1988 I discovered Ecstasy, and for a while, everything changed. I found my place on the dancefloor. That small space became my promised land. My sanctuary. My hideaway. The most beautiful part of it was I could not dance wearing a mask; in those moments the mask melted away. I re-connected with my ten-year-old disco dancing self. That beautiful smiling happy boy who was yet to be beaten, ashamed and angry.

We would dance for hours and welcome in the world. We would hug strangers. Cry at piano breaks. Scream in joy as the beat dropped back in. Soar on the melody and glide down on the off beats. In these moments I caught a glimpse of a future me. Open and loving, trusting myself and others. Hugs. Smiles. Acceptance. Beauty. Love. All of these were mine to give and mine to receive.

When I reminisce, I know that my freedom was only ever temporary. I felt reborn, but once the party was over, I put the mask back on. As long as the music played, I was happy, but in the silence that would envelop me after a party, I would slump into an anxious state. My life began to be an endless cycle of manic, drug-fuelled unmasked mania, followed by fear and anxiety and the clamping on of whatever mask I needed to get me through the day.

The Long Road to Compassion

This hedonistic life could not last forever, and in my early thirties, my life fell apart. I walked away from my home, my job and all of my friends. I stopped partying. My life had spiralled dramatically, and as I looked around at the carnage, I realised that a change was needed. I had become a hollow shell of hard-worn masks. I began to believe the myths and legends I had perpetuated about myself. Fact and fiction began to blur, fantasy and reality melting into each other. For the first time in my life, I could not hide behind a lie. I had to face up to myself and take responsibility.

My mantra became, '*I have caused all of this, and only I can redeem myself.*'

At the age of 33, I retreated into a world of solitude and isolation and for six months lived in an old house with no running water or electricity. I meditated on my life. I read. I ran. I cried. I raged. As I began to nourish my mind and body, I could feel my masks falling away one by one. They were no longer needed. I had no reason to hide. Slowly I pieced myself back together.

I was ready to begin my life again. I moved to Manchester with no plan and no idea what I wanted to do. All I knew was that my eyes were finally opening. I had yet to learn about the masks that some men construct, I had a new curiosity about life and about why I felt and thought the way I did.

Over the next seven years I built a new life away from my family and the village I grew up in. I chose a career that was completely different to running bars. I slowed my life down. I chose nice food and wine over pills and thrills. I chose pubs with log fires over clubs with strobe lights. I chose simple over complicated.

I also chose isolation over integration. Solitude over socialising. At the time I did not notice my retreat from the world, but gradually I whittled my social circle down to a handful of trusted companions. The masks that I constructed allowed me to interact with people with ease. I could don my joker mask, or be a playboy, party animal or old romantic. I even had a philosopher mask for those more cerebral spiritual interactions. I had a jock mask, a music mask, a nerd mask. You name it; I had a mask for it.

Years and years and hardly an authentic expression to call my own, I became a lifelong 'sleight of hand' expert who was suddenly trying to be real. Stripped of my masks, I began to find socialising fraught with anxiety. I did not know who I was or what I believed. I would observe people and wonder at the force of their beliefs. They seemed so sure of themselves. In contrast, I felt like a shadow, without form or focus.

Slowly, however, the seeds of an authentic man were growing. I developed a firm belief in right from wrong. I had opinions that were truly mine and most importantly I began to see that many of my fellow men were experiencing the same disconnect. I began to see inauthenticity everywhere, and it was especially endemic in men. At first, I was repulsed by it, deliberately choosing to shun new male friendships to spare me from their constant banter and bullshit. If it wasn't for my son, then I may well have shunned men for the rest of my days. Thankfully, the universe bestowed upon me the greatest responsibility of my life at 12.22 am on the morning of the 23rd November 2012.

Fatherhood

Fatherhood is the one aspect of my life that feels like the truest essence of who I am and who I always wanted to be. I became a father aged 45. I remember the oddest of sensations as my son slowly floated up to the surface of the birthing pool in North Manchester hospital. It felt like the hole in me had suddenly been filled. What I've realised since that day is that what I felt within me was simply purpose. A new purpose and realisation that I had to grow alongside this new life, embrace this new responsibility and be the best version of myself I could be. From the very first moment I saw my son it felt like coming home.

Through my relationship with him, I began to experience love with trust. What a delicious phrase that is for me. Love with trust. I began to see how closed I had been with my fellow man despite the work I had done to heal myself. My son teaches me something new about the world and myself every day. I've connected with the nurturer inside of me, and for that, I am eternally grateful to him.

As I observed him connect with the world, I began to see the beauty so evident when open-hearted human beings come together. I now know with certainty that we are all here to nurture each other however terrifying that prospect might be. Believe me when I say that sometimes this prospect terrifies me. I am still today capable of closing like a clam in certain situations. I'm only human after all.

Being a father has brought about the firm belief that *all* men must be fathers to themselves *and* others. By this, I mean bringing fatherly energies and behaviours into everyday interactions with other people. Let's all try to be more appreciative of others and accept that we are all different. Let's all be supportive, yet challenge negative behaviours. Let's protect and nurture each other and have fun, *lots* of fun; we needn't take life so seriously.

My son brings me deep joy because he is open, trusting, joyous, and excited. He loves life. The world around him enthrals him. He is always present with his fellow human beings. He *lives* his life. He *loves* his life.

If I had to guess his inner mantra, it would go something like:

'I am here. And I am now.'

And indeed we *all* are.

That is how I intend to live the rest of my life. Here and now.

Reader Notes:

I have a predilection towards managing fear, sadness and shame through the mask of anger. For a long time, I allowed myself to believe that this was a consequence of my upbringing and would never change.

I was wrong.

I now know we all have a choice. We can choose to stay hidden beneath the anger we manifest or we can choose a more empowered path. I chose compassion for myself. I chose to look beyond the anger to the underlying feeling.

Now I see anger not as an expression of how I feel but a cry for help from within myself. My anger is a call to my protector, my 'ego' that says, 'Let me feel what is underneath this. Let me honour what I am feeling.'

Now I listen to that inner voice. What is it telling me? What does it need from me? I now understand that all of my masks were manifestations of my protector 'ego'. Ego built many masks and many walls to keep me safe and separate for a long time.

The thing is, I am human. I need to connect. I need to communicate with integrity and authenticity to be happy. So I have a new purpose.

My job is to tell the truth about me every day. In doing so, I hope that it contributes to the healing of other men who recognise some of their masks in mine.

I see so many masks being worn everyday by the men around me. While these masks may be comfortable to wear, they are spiritually diminishing and take you ever further from your true self.

I want to help other men take their masks off.

About the Author:

Spencer Jacobs is dedicated to inspiring and supporting other men to communicate in healthy ways, particularly during conflict, grief or separation.

He knows personally how difficult it can be as a man to express himself authentically from the heart but is striving to communicate in vulnerability every day, as part of his own healing process.

He is a member of the *Manchester Men's Group* and is a founder of *The Conscious Ramblers* and the *Tomfoolery Club* of North Manchester (whose mission is to have more fun, silliness and great chats)

Spencer is a graduate of The Laughing Horse Comedy Club. He believes in the power of comedy to change men's attitudes to themselves.

His key message is that vulnerability is a strength not a weakness. He has realised from his own experience that it brings about intimacy and connection with others.

He is a student of *A Course in Miracles*, his girlfriend's menstrual cycle and also enjoys reading self-development books about masculinity, anger and loft conversions.

Spencer is a hopeful romantic who lives in Manchester with his son, his psycho kitten and his beautiful and tall girlfriend. He is committed to choosing joy over pain every day.

His hope is that other men will read his story and be inspired to look inside themselves at their own perceptions of what is manhood.

Connect with Spencer:

Email: spencerspeaking67@gmail.com
www.facebook.com/spencerspeaking/manquest

Recommended Resources:

<u>TED Talks:</u>

Justin Baldoni: Why I'm Done Trying to be 'Man Enough'

<u>Books:</u>

Brene Brown: The Power of Vulnerability: Teachings on Authenticity, Connection, & Courage

Lewis Howes: The Mask of Masculinity: How Men Can Embrace Vulnerability, Create Strong Relationships and Live Their Fullest Lives

Robert Moore & Doug Gillette: King, Warrior, Magician, Lover: Rediscovering the Archetypes of the Mature Masculine

Thich Nhat Hanh: Anger: Wisdom for Cooling the Flames

Marshall B Rosenberg: Nonviolent Communication: A Language of Life

Websites:

www.cnvc.org
Facebook: www.facebook.com/sarah-ludford-connect-
with-compassion
Facebook: www.facebook.com/kateyroberts
www.sarahludford.co.uk
www.kateyroberts.com

From Addiction to Recovery
By Shaun Coffey

'Grief can be the garden of compassion. If you keep your heart open through everything, your pain can become your greatest ally in your life's search for love and wisdom.' ~ Rumi

Ever had a dream that you were drowning and struggling for air? That dream felt true to me for much of my childhood and early adulthood. Although in many ways I got to see and do more than most kids, life was rough. Growing up with my dad was hard. He was abusive in all ways, codependent, and living with mental illness. He was diagnosed with bipolar disorder, manic depression, and harboured a tightly kept secret of schizoaffective disorder. Even with all this known to the court and family services, he would eventually end up with custody of me once my parents divorced.

At about seven years old things started to deteriorate. Don't get me wrong, there were times of happiness and joy, though these were often clouded by neglect, physical, emotional and verbal abuse, and abandonment. Living in fear of saying the wrong thing or expressing myself was my reality; you certainly didn't show any emotion in our house. Each day was unpredictable and different things would set off my dad's anger.

I remember one time trying to hide some stuff in a drawer under my bed, during a scheduled room cleaning, and standing to attention in the doorway while my father inspected my room. It wasn't to his satisfaction. He walked in and dumped everything - the dresser drawers, a chest full of toys, and the drawer from under the bed - into the middle of my room. I was ordered to clean it again and not come out of my room until I'd finished. Another time he blacked out while beating me, yet afterwards having no recollection of what he'd done. On another occasion, my dad woke me up with a punch to the face because I'd visited a friend I wasn't supposed to. Things like this continued until I graduated from high school and joined the military.

Joining the United States Marine Corps was one of the scariest yet incredible things I have ever done. I went into boot camp for 13-weeks, took 10-days leave then returned for my official School of Infantry (SOI) training. Within a few weeks of training, I was psychologically assessed. There had been incidents of hazing (harmful, often abusive rituals) going on, with the intent to cause humiliation and toughen us up. One such incident involved being forced to tell 165 men that we wore women's clothing. Other, more punitive incidents I'd prefer not to mention.

I approached the chain of command but the incidents got

worse. In hindsight, the Marine Corps became another version of my father, though on a grander scale. Little wonder that I presented with symptoms of mental illness from PTSD to depression, anxiety and borderline personality disorder during those first few weeks of training.

Being 18, I dealt with it the only way I knew how. I ran hard, and I ran fast. I chose to go AWOL (absent without leave). When I returned, I was put into a legal platoon and told I would be facing bad conduct or dishonourable discharge. Given the opportunity to take liberty (time off), I went AWOL for a second time, this time upgrading my status to a 'deserter'. I would go on to spend 45 days in brigade military prison.

A short time after being released my dad passed away. I got a phone call on April 1, 2001 from my dad's best friend saying he was deteriorating quickly and I should get a flight out there as soon as I could. I knew my dad was sick as he was battling Pulmonary Fibrosis. When I got to the airport, another call came in. My dad was able to speak in between laboured breaths.

'Hey son, how you doing?' he said. My instinct was to break down, but I held my composure.

'I'm good Dad; I'll be there soon. I want you to know that I love you. I understand you did your best and it was good enough. I forgive you.'

He said, 'I love you too '. I received a call about 15 minutes later that he had passed.

My story may paint a picture of a coarse man with rough edges and some significant obstacles in life, but I would like it to be clear that although we had a love-hate relationship, he had moments when he was the father that I needed, and I cherished these moments, even if it meant pushing me away again. My father died aged 48. I was 21. The day after he passed away I called my mom.

My mom and I had a relationship, but it was nowhere near what it could have been. I honestly believed that she didn't care. I saw her a total of around four months, from ages 5 to 21. At 11 and 12 years old, I would call her in secret in the middle of the night, whispering under a blanket hoping my dad wouldn't catch me. I would visit her, and he would call and tell me how much fun he was having and that he wished I was home or that I should come back early. And I did, every time. He knew how to manipulate any scenario to his advantage.

Having to live with everything your father is doing and everything you think your mom isn't, does some crappy things to a young kid's mind. It's little wonder that I would later battle with more mental illness and substance misuse.

The Day That Changed My Life

It was a brisk evening on the east side of Colorado Springs in July 2002. I had been in hiding for a few hours; people were looking for me. At this point in my life, I was what you might call a 'junkie'. I was homeless and had been in a wrong place at the wrong time situation, having spent twenty-five-thousand dollars of my father's fifty-thousand-dollar life insurance policy on drugs. On this day I had gone to the mall with an important guy in our circle. Little did I know this would be the day that would change my life forever.

It was approaching 2:45 pm. The guy offered to take me out because some rumours of foul play were surfacing and he wanted to believe they weren't true. We pulled into the mall car park and entered Macy's department store. Something didn't feel right. It was as if the air was thin and there was tension all over the place. As we walked around the store, he took clothes off the rack and made small talk, expressing the importance of being honest and what it would mean if these rumours were true. After about 25 minutes of shopping, we went to the dressing rooms, and he started putting the articles of clothing on under his regular clothes. At this point, I knew something was wrong. I spoke up about Loss Prevention and mentioned that there were cameras all over the store. Did he listen? No. He told me to pay for a pair of sunglasses and meet him outside.

When I paid for the glasses and made it to the mall exit, he'd vanished. After another 45 minutes of waiting, I called a mutual friend and asked if he had heard from him. Well, now I knew the uneasy feeling I had was no fluke. This friend was my main partner and was also close to the guy in the mall. He was angry, screaming at me and accusing me of setting this whole thing up. It was at this point I knew I was no longer safe. I hung up the phone, called another friend for a ride, and drove about an hour to a 'safe house' where I could collect my thoughts and figure out a plan.

The car ride seemed to take minutes. My mind was racing with thoughts of being in danger. I had an inkling of the type of people they were involved with; three months earlier there'd been a drive-by shooting at a house I was in. I pulled up to an apartment complex and walked down an alleyway filled with open doors and random people, the acrid smell of drugs hanging in the air. I knocked on a door. I was dating a girl at the time who answered it. I quickly explained the events that had happened and told her I needed to stay for a while to figure out what to do next.

In the next 20 minutes, I devised a plan to leave the state and not return. My thoughts were interrupted by the sound of a ringing phone in the next room. I heard my girlfriend pick up and say hello. She quickly walked into the room I was in and looked at me with big terrified eyes, pointing to a closet at the end of the hallway. Panic and fear spread across her face. I knew then to expect the worst. I was going to either hide and live or be found and likely killed. I grabbed my backpack and headed down the hall into the closet.

The closet was pitch black. Jackets were hanging, a vacuum and cleaning supplies were strewn on the floor, and boxes and household items were piled up against the wall. Rapidly I pulled some of the clothing off their hangers, lay in the fetal position and pulled the jackets over the top of me, hugging my backpack for comfort. Up to this point, I didn't even know what was being said on the phone, just that it was severe enough that hiding was a necessity. As the rustling settled everything went silent. Then I heard a faint sound of talking close by. Hearing the voice in the hallway, I recognised it as my girlfriend. She was denying seeing me or knowing where I was. I'd forgotten that they knew where she lived.

There was a knock at the door. I heard the creaking of the hinges as it opened. I could hear a man and woman talking to my girlfriend, asking questions about me in an obvious yet nonchalant way. She played it cool, and after about 10 minutes, they left. I didn't dare move. My leg was starting to go numb; my breath deep but shallow. Everything seemed to be in slow motion.

A few minutes later the closet door opened. My girlfriend

reassured me that everything was ok, the coast was clear. But I couldn't move. Frozen with fear and anxiety, I remained curled in a ball, weeping. She sat down on the floor, put her hand on my head and said, 'You need to be brave, people are looking for you, and you need to go.' I stood up immediately. The only way out was her balcony door. Grabbing the backpack, I tossed it over the railing and leapt to the balcony below and then to the ground.

And then I ran, and I kept running and running. After all, it's what I did best. Four miles later I arrived at a bus station and sat on a bench to collect my thoughts. *This is it. You've hit your bottom, and your life can't get any worse. You're lucky your father isn't here to see this.* Up to this point, my mother had only re-surfaced since my dad's passing. Our relationship was starting to improve. And right now, I needed her more than ever. I pulled out my cell phone and dialled her number.

A soft, brittle voice answered: 'Hello, son. How are you doing?' My eyes filled with tears and my voice broke when I tried to speak. I explained to her that I was in trouble and needed money, a common occurrence in recent months, so she was hesitant. I pleaded with her, begged her to understand and do this one last time. She did. I boarded a bus three hours later.

The Path To Recovery

The need for these events at this point was necessary. Yes, it's a harsh, scary and somewhat unbelievable story; I feel incredibly lucky to be alive. Yet there were still another five years of relapse and recovery before finally getting it. I relapsed after starting a DJ career and got into rave drugs of all kinds that were readily available. This relapse was bad because I didn't discriminate with use; I did whatever was close and lots of it.

July 2018 was 11 years of recovery for me. Having survived these experiences and building from a foundation of mental illness and addiction, I was given an opportunity to switch careers and work with people struggling with substance misuse and mental health disorder, commonly referred to as dual diagnosis treatment. I now work in an Intensive Outpatient facility as a Treatment Coordinator and Peer Recovery Support. Having learned valuable lessons along the way, and finding sobriety a few different times, it has made this career choice the perfect fit. Being able to make a difference in other's lives, showing them that recovery *is* possible and offering them a helping hand in discovering their path, has been one of the most gracious, humbling and rewarding experiences of my life.

During my drug use, I didn't recognise warning signs or learn from top programs or rehab facilities. I honestly never knew they existed when I was getting clean and had no one to direct me toward it, so I did it mostly by myself. Being able to work alongside the clinical team at my work has been amazing. I've co-facilitated group sessions, accompanied clients to court and various other appointments, and have learned so much about myself along the way. Up until recently, my work was an all-female intensive outpatient program, I am also the only male on staff. Working closely with these women has been a blessing. As previously mentioned, I hadn't connected with my mom very much in my earlier years, and for a significant part of my life, struggled with trauma, abandonment, depression, and post-traumatic stress disorder surrounding that. I had also associated drug use and mental health as negative parts of my life. Despite initial reservations about bringing me on to the team, the women have supported me unconditionally. There were concerns that a trauma response could be triggered, or that girls on the programme may not respond well to me, but my colleagues believed in me. In the year that I've worked there I have done more self-exploration and skill building than ever before. The clinicians have helped me understand that being in recovery and working a recovery program are similar but different. I now understand why my brain works the way it does and when to divert emotion or when to speak. I understand that sarcasm and jokes – my defence mechanism - have their place. We know that a drug is a drug; if we can unlock the why, the 'what' will lose its power.

We are put in situations that life and the universe know we can handle. The only time we learn anything about our true self is when we face adversity or defeat, fear and sadness. My relationship with my father was rough and taught me to hide emotion and knowing this - after therapy, medication, and a lot of self-exploration - I've been able to find a balance. I have become more empathic, studied a little metaphysics and mediumship and have found my 'ground'.

Today, my relationship with my mom and stepfather is amazing. We have now built a strong foundation to work from, and they are two people I admire and respect so much. They have been pivotal in me getting sober and staying clean. I believe it happened this way for a reason. I'm glad we have been able to connect and continue to grow, daily.

Men typically find themselves in situations where feeling and showing emotions is taboo or not socially accepted. We become 'like women' to our male friends, ridiculed for showing weakness or emasculated for public displays of emotion. Often, we can't show emotion in our homes or around our families; that was certainly true of my upbringing. And when we repress our emotions, we stay stuck, our inner world implodes, while our outer world often collapses around us.

The ultimate lesson I have learned throughout life is that I need to stop being afraid of what can or might go wrong and focus on what is going right! The first step in getting somewhere is to acknowledge that you're no longer willing to stay where you are. I will forever be grateful to the incredible people who have helped me change and make progress in my life. In the words of Tony Robbins: 'Change happens when the pain of staying the same, becomes greater than the pain of making a change.'

If you are reading this and struggling with mental health or substance use disorders, know that recovery and stability *are* possible. Find a way to reconnect to the true you beneath the facade, and if you are having trouble with that, please reach out. Talk to someone and let them know you want help. Tell someone you are depressed or have debilitating mental health or substance abuse going on. It's ok for us to cry. It's ok for us to be vulnerable. Today I am free from the many shackles that once weighed me down. Believe in the you before the addiction, believe in the people who believe in you. Make a pact with yourself to live footstep by footstep and find a pathway to recovery. Your loved ones believe in you. I believe in you. You are worth it!

Reader Notes:

At the start of writing this chapter, I thought, *wow, this is a great opportunity to get my story out there and some awareness wrapped around addiction, mental health and recovery.* It started great, and a couple of weeks later hell broke loose.

I had both professional and personal deaths that affected me in ways I've never experienced. I couldn't focus in school and withdrew from the semester. I hung out with people who don't have an addiction disorder and, consequently, can do things without reservation. I think when we get so caught up in life and the happenings around us, we sometimes forget about the small choices we make that derail us from being happy or successful. We accept that because of our actions or circumstances, we deserve the negative consequences. We're stuck in a world where we cannot progress or move forward, and we do this to ourselves.

After this chapter was finished, the past was drudged up, and the tears were cried. The realisation came that I *am* good enough, that every experience has built, shaped or moulded me into who I am today. Not for one second would I go back and change any portion of my life. Today I may be broken with glued together pieces. I may have PTSD, anxiety, depression and a personality disorder. I may fall on my face repeatedly, making mistakes over and over again. But one thing I don't have any more is fear. I am not afraid to express myself. I am not afraid to show my emotions, and actively encourage other men to be vulnerable. I am not afraid to fail. I am not afraid to make mistakes.

You needn't live with your emotions and feelings bottled up. Learn or seek ways to grow. Free your mind from negative and unhelpful thoughts. Ask for help. I've shared my story to reach those who are struggling or having similar experiences. Whether your family is affected by the disease, whether you have parents living with substance misuse or perhaps you personally are struggling, know this to be true: there is always hope. Continue to love and support those affected. Break away from the stigma. And be a part of the solution.

About the Author:

Shaun is a Certified Peer Recovery Support Worker in the State of New Hampshire, US and father to a 7-year-old daughter. He is currently working as a public speaking for schools, corporate, and nonprofit events, sharing his story of addiction to recovery and is working on building web and social media platforms for that. Shaun has uncovered a love for running and is currently training for the Richmond VA Marathon and looking into a 50-mile ultra-marathon trail race. He loves the mountains, photography and living in the moment. Shaun has a goal of becoming a Licensed Alcohol and Drug Counselor, and furthering his career in the Substance Use Disorder field.

Connect with Shaun:

Email: coffey.shaun@gmail.com
Facebook: www.facebook.com/shaun.zyon.coffey

Recommended Resources:

<u>Books:</u>

Mind Hacking: How to Change Your Mind For Good in 21 Days.

<u>Websites:</u>

www.fitnh.org
www.samhsa.org

Facing My Demons
By Andy Bowker

'There is much about our experience as men that can only be shared with, and understood by, other men. There are stories we can tell only to those who have wrestled in the dark with the same demons and been wounded by the same angels. Only men understand the secret fears that go with the territory of masculinity.' ~ Sam Keen, Fire in the Belly

C hildhood is supposed to be wonderful and free. But I was different. I was locked in my own little world and barely spoke to anyone. While many of my school peers were interacting with each other and forming friendships, I spent many school playtimes alone. I was the outcast. I probably displayed traits on the autism spectrum and had a particular obsession with football and football statistics. I was picked on and bullied. People didn't like me. This exclusion cut deep and left me with a paralysing fear of rejection, which has held me back in friendships, relationships, career and life in general ever since.

My mind formed many subconscious patterns and beliefs during my childhood, mostly negative. I had virtually no self-worth. After a very dark period of my life, I turned to Christianity, having been brought up going to church.

Christianity helped keep some intense emotions at bay, but I completely lost myself in the process. I believed I was a sinner who had been saved from hell only by Jesus dying on the cross. And so I became fixated on obeying God, rather than thinking for myself, for fear of retribution. I was committed to my church: I played the saxophone there most Sundays, read the Bible almost daily and was supposedly a good Christian. I appeared to have good moral standards.

However, denial and unprocessed trauma had built up over the years, and I was anything but my true self. I'd already experienced one severe breakdown in 2001 when I thought my life would end; somehow I recovered. Instead of being a turning point, little did I know that life would take a turn for the worse.

Living in Fear

In 2006 my world came crashing down. My thoughts had become more extreme. I believed I was damned to hell forever and could not see a way out. I thought I had betrayed Jesus and even occasionally wondered if I was the antichrist. The Bible seemed to confirm that I was condemned. I spent a month in hospital then moved in with my parents; I couldn't expect anyone else to support me given my mental state.

This whole period lasted around six months. I didn't want to live, but suicide was not an option as I was scared as to what might await me in the 'afterlife'. I knew that my time as a Christian was over and officially renounced my faith during this period. I would read articles of people who had abandoned Christianity and were now okay, which gave me a brief glimmer of hope. But I was still plagued by condemnation, fear and terror. To this day, I'm not entirely sure how I survived. Christianity had initially saved me, and I couldn't have imagined life without it when I was a Christian, yet now I felt imprisoned by darkness and despair, trapped inside a shell of a man, feeling frightened and dead inside.

I am sure that a higher power of some sort was watching over me. The hell I went through was so horrendous that it could have destroyed me. I know people had been praying for me and maybe that helped.

Then I had an epiphany. I came across a support website for ex-Christians and posted my story and what had happened. I felt the love and support from other members who replied to me; I felt hopeful. I started questioning the belief that I was going to hell. And then, like dominoes, all of the religious paradigms collapsed around me. For the first time, it all became clear. I was *not* going to hell. I was *not* the sinner I thought. *Maybe I could think for myself and live life on my terms. Maybe life was giving me a second chance.*

A Fresh Start

From my breakdown came my breakthrough. I felt freer than I had in years. I decided to move away from my hometown in Dorset, heading 275 miles north to Leeds. It was a huge risk – leaving my job, family and the familiarity of what I knew - but I needed a fresh start. I needed to start *living* again. Risks are there to be taken in times like these!

I swiftly lost my first job in Leeds, learning a huge lesson in how *not* to communicate via email, and so took on a succession of temporary assignments. The recession soon followed. It became more difficult to find work. When I did re-enter the workplace, I found the work and environment incredibly stressful. In one particular job, I spent the weekends recovering from stress and dreading work every day. This was no way to live.

While in this job, I found out that my brother had died very suddenly. I immediately headed south to spend time with my parents. My boss, with whom I had a good relationship, was overworked and started piling more work on top of my already insane workload just a month after my brother's death. So I quit.

The next year was one of uncertainty and somewhat of a blur. I joined a meditation group to help me get back on track and to move through the grief of my brother's death in my own way. I couldn't have gone through an intense grieving process that some people do; that would have pushed me over the edge. I do my best to honour my brother's memory and trust that he is in a good place now.

Asking for Help

Sometimes it can take a crazy situation to get men to speak out and ask for help. That was certainly true of me. After my second breakdown, I stopped giving a fuck about whether or not it was 'manly' to display emotions. Nevertheless, I still find it difficult to cry, even though I know it's healthy. For men, opening their heart isn't easy – we're taught to be stoic and emotionally detached - and it's certainly felt like a long and arduous journey to shed old behaviours and beliefs that have kept me stuck.

I tried for a while to overcome my issues by myself, with the help of my book reading habit. I always had the excuse that I didn't have enough money for therapy, and perhaps I felt that my issues were so unique that no-one would understand me or could help me. I meditated. I tried my best to be spiritual, to surrender and let go. I even tried to kid myself that my fears and subconscious beliefs were 'not real'. But whatever I did, the issues causing me pain were still there.

That said, books and videos from many wise people were

a huge help. *The Power of Now* by Eckhart Tolle showed me the concept of living in the present moment, something I'd never previously considered, so consumed was I by the fears that kept my head in the future. But the most important thing I've learnt along my journey is that pain doesn't disappear by fighting or denying it and that it's okay to feel what we perceive to be negative emotions. So often – particularly within modern spirituality - we think that we should be feeling happy and positive all the time and not struggle. Or that somehow we awaken and are immune from suffering. Yet *all* of our emotions are part of the human experience, part of what *makes* us human. Acceptance and being real about where you're at, right now, is fundamental to healing. Feeling *is* healing. And being fully present to our experience in *this* moment, no matter what the discomfort, is what enables us to walk through the darkness towards the light.

That doesn't make things easy, however. My journey has been one of deep pain, grief, trauma, heartache and confusion. Friendships and, in particular, relationships have been difficult. My confidence with women bombed at an early age, and I've lived with an awful fear of rejection as a result. I've had very little in the way of romantic relationships which still hurts, and I struggle with this daily. More recently I've started to dive deeper into the pain surrounding this, and it seems that there is layer upon layer to uncover. It's important to work on how you feel within yourself rather than looking outwardly towards other men, women and society.

I have also started to get help from other people and connect with more like-minded folk. Particularly if you have deep rooted trauma, you won't heal on your own. There is a reason why we seldom discuss trauma in mainstream society, and why medication is so readily handed out for depression and anxiety. While I agree that medication can be beneficial – and necessary – for some, people often want the quickest and easiest way out. And trauma is bloody hard to face. If you're anything like me, you'll have encountered resistance to facing your demons. You may have closed down at times and found other ways to numb - or avoid - the pain. And that's okay. You're doing your best with what you've learnt and the resources available to you. Show yourself compassion and take comfort in knowing that there *is* another way.

First Steps to Healing

If you have suffered, it probably won't be a straight and easy path to healing. What matters is that you have a willingness to face your demons, your resistance, your closed heart, and your temptation to give up. Even if things seem to be moving slowly, don't try and force yourself to heal. It generally takes time.

It can take a lot to crack a man open, and if I hadn't had

such a crazy life experience, maybe I would have remained closed. Having had two breakdowns which could have easily destroyed me, I feel grateful that life has given me another chance.

The journey to self-love is a strange one for me at times, given my strong sense of lack that stems from childhood. Certain thought patterns frequently run on repeat in my mind. It's easy to think that I'll be happy when I meet the 'love of my life' or when I am living a life of freedom. One thing I have learnt is that I can't force myself to feel any better, any more than I can force someone to be my friend. Just because you're not 'healed' and still having bad days doesn't mean you are doing anything wrong.

The toughest part of the healing journey is facing your demons. And embracing them rather than running away. The prospect of this can be terrifying. Most of us carry a lot of unhealed emotional baggage, and subconsciously we fear that our pain would overwhelm us if we came face to face with it. Men, in particular, aren't taught how to deal with emotions, instead learning to suppress or project them. Many of us turn to alcohol and try to be strong and silent for fear of being seen as weak.

One of the most critical things for me is to be discerning about who I allow into my life. I would never tolerate anyone who slandered me for expressing my truth and sharing my experiences, as I have in this chapter, for instance. Friendships with like-minded people are crucial; you needn't embark on this journey alone. And this journey starts with you. In a culture where withdrawal and rejection are typical childhood punishment, it's natural for many of us to fear the judgement of others as adults. I hear so often that men are scared of telling their family, their partners or others that they are struggling. We can put a stop to this story.

The patriarchy will only dismantle if men step fully into their power and vulnerability, and are willing to deal with their shit. It means asking for help. It means dropping the tough exterior and pretence that you have it all together. It means not buying into social stereotypes about what it means to be a man and to start reclaiming the essence of who you are beneath the labels.

It's fair to say that men have less support available than women, and sometimes it can feel like a lonely journey. The collective pain of men is huge, and the emotional suppression of males from an early age is, in my opinion, the most harmful thing that has ever happened to men, and needs to end. Sometimes I wonder if the lid will truly be taken off the collective pain that men feel.

Facing our deeper wounds is an ongoing daily practice; generations of pain deeply entrenched in our psyche and DNA doesn't heal overnight. Tormented by our mind - which is already in overdrive constantly trying to solve problems – we tend to overthink. For me, it's about getting out of my head and into my heart; yoga has been a game changer. It's important to find a practice that helps you stay grounded and quietens the mind. You cannot stop having thoughts, but you can observe your thoughts without getting stuck in them.

No matter what society dictates about how to be a man, no matter what 'truths' spiritual folks tell you about masculinity, you can only be vulnerable and authentic when you embody *your* truth. You can be soft and gentle or macho, so long as who you be is authentic to you. We are all different. We each have different gifts and experiences to bring to this world.

When men start to come together and support one another, when we open up and share our struggles, and when we commit to healing from the inside out, the world will become more beautiful.

Reader notes:

Men have been conditioned for generations to hide their pain. Are you willing to break the cycle, no matter how difficult it may be?

We cannot heal on our own. While we *do* ultimately heal ourselves – no one has the power to do it for us - we need support to get us there. Ask for help; it's a strength, not a weakness.

It can be extremely hard for men to live a heart-centred life due to societal rules and expectations of what a man should be. Are you ready and willing to do the deeper work, to face your demons head on and leave a legacy of authenticity for future generations?

About the Author:

Andy has emerged from some very dark times and is determined to be the best version of himself, after years of trying to be someone he wasn't. He is a keen writer, photographer, walker, traveller and musician, and believes that yoga is life changing.

He desires to see more people, particularly men, be real about how they feel, and understand that it *is* possible to face your demons without being annihilated in the process. He believes that you don't have to be anywhere near perfect to be worthy of living your best life. He has had a lot of resistance to opening up and it has taken a lot to get him where he is today; honesty about where you are at is key.

Andy currently resides in Yorkshire on the edge of the beautiful Yorkshire Moors and also spends time in Manchester connecting with like-minded souls.

Connect with Andy:

Email: andybowker74@gmail.com

Facebook:
www.facebook.com/andybowker74
www.facebook.com/AndysCorner74

Recommended Resources:

Books:

The Deepest Acceptance: Radical Awakening in Ordinary Life by Jeff Foster

The Power of Acceptance by Annemarie Postma

The Untethered Soul by Michael A Singer

Reasons To Stay Alive by Matt Haig

Websites:

www.lifewithoutacentre.com - Jeff Foster's website.

www.remakingmanhood.com - A highly recommended resource for men.

www.rickfortier.me - Another man who is doing great work.

www.facebook.com/SOULSHAPING - Jeff Brown's
Facebook page.

Boys Do Cry
By Brad Kenny

"Grief can be the garden of compassion. If you keep your heart open through everything, your pain can become your greatest ally in your life's search for love and wisdom." ~ Rumi

In April 27, 1964, I was born as the third child of a devout Catholic family. My identical twin brother followed 3-minutes later. Early life was unsettling as our family relocated cross-country frequently. By the time I was two, we'd moved seven times. I have only one memory before five years of age, and it was when I was two and looking at my newborn brother Phillip as he slept on the couch. He later died of SIDS (Sudden Infant Death Syndrome). My mother never forgave herself for that, eternally blaming herself for his death. She would carry this with her until she died.

Life was fairly typical of a Catholic family as I understand it. Blessed to be raised with corporal punishment, my brothers and I received a generous share. I grew up chastened for expressing my emotions, learning that it wasn't safe to feel any emotion, especially sadness or disappointment.

'Stop crying, or I'll give you something to cry about!' was routinely heard within my household, swiftly followed up with the 'something'.

As a Catholic family, we were required to eat together. Mom would make breakfast, lunch or dinner; we'd set the table, say grace, then eat. From the outset this all seemed civilised; we were the model Catholic family. As typically happened during most meals, Mom would find something to get upset about and start screaming and shouting at my dad. Typically this resulted in her throwing her coffee cup and cutlery at him; or whatever was close by. I was later told by one of my brothers that she'd stabbed him once. Another time we were driving home from church and a row ensued. My mom took the keys out of the ignition and threw them out the window - while the car was in motion. Never a dull moment.

Violence was an almost daily occurrence. I can count on one hand how many good (happy, carefree, stress-free, non-violent) days we had. Despite this, we never wanted for anything; our material needs were always met. Life was one great Catholic-guilt induced paradox.

I grew up with a fear of my mom and consequently the fear of love from women. I strongly believed that women (and men) would either betray or abandon me. I say men because my dad *did* eventually leave. He did it in epic fashion too, which I will talk about later. My mom regularly accused my dad of cheating and being an alcoholic. Looking back, I have no idea whether this was true as I was too young to know what all that meant. He is in recovery now, so perhaps it was.

We moved to California into an amazing magical house that felt like a multi-level fort. The yelling, screaming and hitting continued; kids need consistency, after all. Tension escalated daily. One time my mom left for three days without a word or hint as to where she was going. On her return, a more volatile fight ensued, this time my father the one to walk out the door. When he came back, we children were each taken separately and asked who we wanted to live with. I was confused and scared to think of what was happening to my family. Nevertheless, the decision was made for us one day when my mom, brothers and I returned from the grocery store to discover some strangers leaving our house.

As it transpired, it was no longer *our* house. It was theirs. They'd just bought it. My dad had sold the house from under our nose. This is where I learned about abandonment in grand fashion. From that point, it was clear to me that if my dad could leave at the drop of a hat, how easy would it be for anyone to leave with no communication? In my mind, I would never be safe from the hurt of someone leaving without warning.

Fortunately, our uncle gave us a place to stay until we

found our own home. He was a nice guy and had a good job and no children. Tragically he later committed suicide after going back to school to get a geo-engineering degree yet finding no work as an older man re-entering the workforce.

Losing My Way

I remember always trying to find someone to be a guide for me. Someone to show me what it means to be a man, how to love, how to treat people. The only examples I'd had were of abuse, abandonment and betrayal; little wonder that I found it difficult to trust and get close to people. I had no idea what boundaries were and how to respect them; for myself or others. This led to the end of many relationships.

In middle school, I got into a fight on the very first day. I thought I was a badass when it took only one punch to knock him down, though this didn't serve to impress my crush who turned out to be his sister. My mother was a regular at every school and knew every principal on a first name basis due to my behaviour. They really should have given her a parking spot. One of the school counsellors took an interest in our family and convinced my mom he was a decent guy, persuading her to let me and my brothers stay overnight at his place. He and his roommate ended up getting high and trying to molest us. This wasn't the type of guidance I'd had in mind.

We moved to Seattle and ended up renting a home in the Ballard section of town. Before starting high school, I discovered a love for marijuana and thus began a period of getting stoned before school each morning and each afternoon once I returned home. One day, when I was 16, my mom was doing what she did with her preferred method of delivering her message through discipline. I realised I was taller than her and no longer willing to tolerate her abuse. I stood up to her and told her she would never hit me again. She never did. The screaming, however, continued on a regular basis until I moved out at the age of 18.

I ended up moving back in with my mom on the agreement that I would go to college, something I'd resisted. Even though my grades showed I was smart (I had also received a Grant to go to school that required no repayment), I had no idea what I wanted to do. I had no focus and no direction. Eventually, I dropped out of college and was consequently ordered to leave home. I found a place to live and continued my job as a manager at McDonald's. By this point, I was severely depressed and having suicidal thoughts regularly. At 2 am one morning, I called my mom and asked her to come and get me. She took me home, and I went to bed. I couldn't sleep so went to the ER at Harborview Hospital. They did my intake and then handcuffed me to a gurney, fearing that I might do myself some harm. A male doctor took me into an examination room and gave me a full physical. He asked for my number so he could follow up with me. And follow up with me he did.

Knowing I'd had no father figure since a young age, he presented himself to be a mentor and suggested we go fishing together. The doctor took me to a secluded place by a river and suggested we get naked. I declined. Later in the hotel room when he put on some porn and again suggested we get naked, I refused. Another example of putting my trust in someone only to be let down.

The Life of a Lothario

I went to counselling and slowly started piecing my life back together. Around the same time, my mother had one last chance to accept a promotion, having already turned it down several times. We moved to the suburbs of Chicago. A fresh start! I threw myself back into school and never looked back. I made the Dean's List twice and graduated in 1989.

Right now you might be thinking, 'Ok; *he finally got himself figured out.*' No. I proceeded to become a world-class womaniser. I convinced myself that I was looking for a deep and meaningful relationship yet, in reality, didn't allow anyone into my heart. No one came close to cracking me open. The problem was that I had no idea what a loving, authentic and safe relationship looked like, not to mention that I'd never been able to trust anybody fully. I was a blind man trying to drive a car. Consequently, I ended up hurting too many people, mostly myself. Validation and positive attention was coming from women all the time. But I didn't know what to do with it.

At 28, I married my first wife. She was beautiful and genius level intelligent. The best thing about her were her two children. Before getting married, we ended our relationship seven times. On the final break-up – crunch time - I decided to get married for the sake of her kids so that they could have a father figure, as their biological dad was fairly absent (he later made up for lost time and became an amazing dad). I was very immature, and marrying her for her kids was a bad decision. I needed a ton of attention; attention that I didn't receive as a child. It was never enough. I always needed more. I never cheated on her in the physical sense, but I did cross boundaries more times than I care to admit. We went through some rough times, and I eventually called it quits in July of 2004.

I thought I had it all figured out when I met my second wife. It was not to be. The truth is, she wasn't that into me. I remember spending nights alone, crying when she would stay out until 2, 3 or 4 am with no idea of where she was. *Why didn't she want to stay home with me?* I asked her to make me – us - a priority. She travelled for work, and when she would come home having been on the road for several days or weeks, I hoped we'd rip each other's clothes off and reconnect. It didn't happen. She was always too tired. I'd beg for her attention. Weekend after weekend of her promises to make us a priority - of making *me* a priority - were followed by her sitting on the couch all weekend playing computer games. My friends told me she was cheating on me and I chose not to go down the road of looking for evidence. It all made sense though: no sex, no emotional investment in me or the relationship, and an endless list of broken promises. I should have walked away.

I was desperate to feel wanted, loved and appreciated. My wife and I went seven or eight months without sex, so I hooked up with an old friend, hoping that somehow my wife would someday fall back in love with me. To me, it was only sex, and I loved my wife. My thought was, *I have needs, and she refuses to meet them. So while I wait for her, I will find someone who understands and can support my situation.*

My wife found out that I'd cheated and the marriage ended soon after. We were married and divorced within three years.

My next partner was beautiful, the smartest person I had ever met: honest, kind, giving, and all the things I was looking for in a relationship. By now, I had made a lot of progress with self-awareness through years of counselling and a determination to be a better person. We had a good relationship, a good sex life and everything I could wish for. However, this still wasn't enough to stop my roving eye, and I was unfaithful. Again. I began going to SLAA (Sex & Love Addicts Anon) 12 step meetings. There I discovered I wasn't a sex addict but desired to be non-monogamous. I started living the life of someone who had an 'open' relationship. Only, I failed to discuss with my partner.

One night, my partner discovered a text to my SLAA sponsor telling him I had to confess to being unfaithful. Confronted with the evidence, I had no choice but to confess to her. She had made it very clear that sharing was against her beliefs by a method I was very familiar with: hitting. When I'd made that confession, every woman I had ever hurt manifested in her eyes and the pain was unbearable. I promised myself and the Universe I would never to do it again. I have kept that promise.

We stayed in contact and eventually got back together a few months later. My partner suggested we have an 'open' relationship. In my heart, I knew it wouldn't work. I knew she was only trying to appease me and find some way to stay together. Against my better judgement, we reconciled. I wanted to prove how much I loved her, that I would remain faithful and was truly repentant for what I had done.

We bought a house together, and I hoped she would see

how committed I was. Well, it was never enough, and we fought regularly. She would say very hurtful things followed by, 'I'm sorry. I know you're doing everything I asked of you. I just can't let go of what happened.' I didn't blame her. And when she returned from a visit to her mom's demanding that we sell the house because she 'hated the neighbourhood' and 'hated the yard', I knew it was the end. She had said these things so many times, and no matter what she said, all I heard was, 'I regret getting back together with you.'

The Purge

I moved out, purchased my own house then went to San Diego to attend a leadership course.

It. Changed. My. Life.

I'd done 15 years of counselling so that I could be more honest, communicative, and accountable in relationships, yet despite this, my heart remained closed. I went through the course and purged all the hurt and betrayal that I had committed, and that had been committed against me. I looked at how my parents' behaviour moulded me and the stories I'd made up and had been carrying throughout my life. And then I cried. For 20 out of 90 days. 49 years worth of bottled, pent-up emotions, releasing a long history of unprocessed trauma and pain. I also learned to open my heart after a lifetime of protecting it and building a wall to keep others away.

I have since taken more transformation and self-empowerment courses to build my emotional intelligence, self-awareness and make myself a stronger person. I look for ways to get uncomfortable, so I can have more awareness of what others around me are experiencing.

I am now at a place where I openly cry in front of friends and am known for being one of the first men to cry in a room, and I have zero shame in doing so. When I went through the course, the thing I most heard was that my self-expression gave everyone else permission to dig deep and allow themselves to feel everything. I wish I could say it was easy, but it was extremely difficult. There were days where my brain refused to shut down. I went many nights of getting little to no sleep. There was one stretch where I went three nights straight with no sleep. I thought I was one more crazy thought from being batshit crazy and never coming back. I had to have a 'come to Jesus' talk with myself. I could either continue to try and 'think my way through' my issues and go crazy, or I could allow myself to 'feel' everything and go crazy. Either way, I was fucked. I decided to do something different. I finally allowed myself to get messy, to open up, to cry. Now I've reached where I am today; a man who can allow himself to feel it all and know I can handle it. While I am far from perfect, my journey has given me the gifts of compassion and understanding, and I use them with my clients every day.

I continue my journey of self-discovery and giving back. I volunteer for the organisation that supported me by helping others as they go through their own process to master their emotions and be better versions of themselves. And I now help others step into deeper, more meaningful relationships by guiding them into a more loving and accepting relationship with themselves.

It's okay to cry and get messy. Emotions have no gender bias; they're human emotions available to us all. Whatever life has thrown at you, whatever unprocessed pain you're carrying, I'm proof that it's never too late to break the cycle and start a whole new chapter of your life.

About the Author:

Brad Kenny is an experienced Life and Relationship coach who is passionate about what he does. His childhood was filled with physical, emotional and verbal abuse and what that taught his was that love is paramount to everything.

His calling is to support and guide women to re-imagine their life and break free of thoughts an behaviours that undermine them. His direct, compassionate and honest approach will support you in reaching your goals.

As a trained and experienced Life Coach, he has the tools

and understanding to support and guide women to create the life they imagine and get a renewed sense of self. He will work with you so that you can have the relationship of your dreams and find your next great love.

Recommended Resources:

Websites:

Leadership Course Mentioned: www.alasandiego.com

Books:

Attached: The New Science of Adult Attachment And How It Can Help You Find - And Keep- Love by Amir Levine, M.D. & Rachel S. F. Heller, M.A.

How To Break Your Addiction To A Person by Howard M. Halpern, PhD

No More Mr. Nice Guy: A Proven Guide For Getting What You Want In Love, Sex & Life by Dr. Robert A. Glover

Finding My Way Home
By Richie Nelson

'Our scientific power has outrun our spiritual power. We have guided missiles and misguided men.' ~ Martin Luther King, Jr.

I remember my childhood before 'life' happened. I had an innate sense of spiritual and emotional knowing; how life should 'feel'.

I had a deep connection with myself and the universe. I felt safe and at home in my body.

I could 'be' myself. Soft. Cheeky. Empathic. Caring. Gentle. Loving. Playful. Curious.

Innocent.

I would sit for hours pondering life in the shower. On the toilet. At the beach. I would watch people interact and know what they were saying. Even if I couldn't hear them, I could predict what they would do.

These memories are like a psychedelic, lucid dream. They have a familiar feeling attached to them. Like remembering your home or returning to your home. Like a sense of universal belonging.

In these memories, I remember feeling free from worry, drama, judgment, blame, anger, sadness, fear and criticism. It felt good to belong to something bigger. But life began to change - rapidly - and that feeling of being 'home' or belonging disappeared.

I found myself alone, sucked into reality, my first 'disconnected' memory being my first day at school. I remember sitting on the front steps of my primary school crying for my mother, unsure what I was meant to do with myself.

That moment sums up how the next ten years felt. Cut off from 'home'. Disconnected from anything familiar. No guidance on how to fit in, at school, or in this world. No guidance on how to make friends or become a man.

Mum and Dad were arguing a lot. I just wanted everyone to get along! I felt the need to protect my mother. This is how I became a 'fixer'. I made the decision it was my responsibility to keep the peace and keep the family together.

Anger seemed unworldly to me. *Why couldn't we all get along?*

I got myself so wound up trying to keep the peace that I landed myself in the hospital with stomach migraines. Physically crippling anxiety before the age of ten. Nice.

When Mum ran away from my father, taking my brothers and me with her, things got worse. She told us we were just popping out somewhere, but it turned out to be a lie. We ended up changing schools and disappearing from our normal lives. I wasn't allowed to speak to my father.

We lived out of a women's shelter for six months without enough money or food. We'd gone from luxury to rock bottom overnight. I remember being able to call my dad on my birthday for one minute and then being told to hang up on him.

I'll never forget how sad my dad sounded, or how much I cried that night. He didn't know where we were. He couldn't do anything. *I* couldn't do anything. Mum was doing her best.

Imagine being this intuitive, emotional boy without his dad, living with a group of fearful women. Every single person in that shared house - several families – were victims of drug abuse and domestic violence. My mum, myself, and two brothers all slept in one room listening to the other families scream and yell at each other.

Why did my mum bring us here? How was this better than with dad?

It made no sense at the time. No one explained it to me. What was I to do with all these feelings and thoughts?

So I did what society tells us. I got angry. I took my power back in the only way I knew how. I began running away from Mum. Getting angry at school. Getting into fights. Smoking. Stealing. Escaping into my Game Boy games. I was still only 9 years old.

Mum didn't seem to have it together. I remember her not being home, and me needing to make noodles for my brothers for dinner. I was a kid, trying to be a parent. A little boy carrying the weight of the world on his shoulders, with absolutely no guidance or role models. And I had a shit load of feelings that were building up with nowhere to go.

In 5th grade, we were upgraded to a transition home. It was nice; we had our own space to be a family. The blood stains around the house, in the bedding and mattresses, were questionable. Bad shit must have happened there.

Again, I asked, 'Why are we here in this filthy house? Where's my dad?'

No answers. Nothing that made sense.

I started to run away. Mum and I had a big argument after I returned from a weekend with my dad. A really fucking good weekend too. We had fun. Not a worry in the world. When I returned home, Mum was in a flurry of emotions. Rush. Worry.

And she was cooking meatballs. Those meatballs became the staple from hell. We would be eating meatballs for the next month. She also wanted us to go to church. Jesus had a big role in breaking my family apart, at least, that's what I'd learned from my father. So I rebelled.

'No more meatballs. No more Jesus. Fuck Meatballs and Jesus! Fuck you, Mum! I want to live with my dad!'

So I ran away from home again, a little boy crying his eyes out and ducking into side streets to hide from the police. It was like a horrible movie.

My dad found me in the middle of the main road. The police had notified him I had run away again. This time he finally found me. It felt like he saved me. Little did I know how much at that moment I had saved him.

Living with Dad felt 'lighter'. I got quality time I had never gotten with him before. I refused to go back to Mum's, and eventually, Dad got custody of all three of us boys. I didn't see my mum for more than a few minutes over the next decade.

Learning to Fit In

As I grew older, I usually had one close friend but seldom fit into a 'group'. I thought this was something I wanted. So I decided to fit in. I was sick of being a loner, getting bullied, constantly crying and feeling disempowered. I used anger as the fuel. It was better than being sad. I began to dress like the 'cool kids'. Talk like them. Walk like them.

And I did it better.

Not only could I get good grades (I was, and still am, proudly a massive nerd) but I was confident with girls too.

It seemed if you could get a girlfriend and get laid, you were accepted by the other boys. This made you a 'man'. I saw my dad constantly with women. Driven by money, fancy cars, and a *fuck you* attitude. The cool kids at school did the same thing. So I got myself a girlfriend. I got laid. I got a job. I got money. I began to tell the world FUCK YOU.

I pushed down the soft, wise, spiritual little boy inside of me. In all of this time, it never felt *right*. It never felt like *me*. But this new identity I invented gave me a sense of connection, belonging, power and control. The pressure and aggression that I felt from my father and boys at school became a way of life.

Hustling

I began juggling high school with working for Dad on my weekends and holidays. I was his son, employee, a supportive ear and an emotional punch bag. I was forced to grow up really fucking fast.

I wouldn't trade the stress of this upbringing. It gave me my gifts. But it nearly broke me.

Trying to be who he and society wanted me to be was wrong. Trying to be this overly charged, overly masculine dude with a 'fuck you' attitude when I was *not* that guy didn't sit right.

Looking back, it makes sense why I escaped into unhealthy relationships, sex, became a wannabe playboy, got hooked on medication, drugs, alcohol, smoking, spent all the money I earned, and frequently got into trouble. The more I hustled and pushed my feelings down, the bigger the hole in me grew. And I could not fill it!

In 2011, I went on a trip to Bali with a few of 'the boys'. When I returned, my perspective had shifted for good. I had seen there was more to life than just working, getting married, buying a house and dying.

I remember having a screaming match with Dad at work, breaking down crying, saying, 'If this is a family business, why is it that all we do is work? How come we don't do any family stuff anymore? What's the point of working our lives away if we can't enjoy being a family?'

In that moment, I had uncovered a truth. But the moment was fleeting.

We continued to hustle and grind. Argue and torment. Every minute of every day was a life spent walking on eggshells. I became so intuitive from having to meet this emotional demand, but it was too much. I had no way to protect my energy. I didn't know who or what I was. I felt like I was crazy, and the only way to cope was to self-medicate and escape. It was the only way to 'get back home'.

In 2012, I went overseas to Thailand to get away. I fell ill, caught a tummy bug and within 12 hours was hurling blood up like something out of *The Shining*. Vomiting blood like that scares the hell out of you. It was at this point that shit got real.

The doctors said they would put a camera down my throat. 'Basic procedure,' they said. But they didn't put me to sleep correctly. It took four or five of them to hold me down as they stuffed the tubing down my throat. I felt myself choking. Suffocating. Fighting for air.

I felt the loss of control of my body. I felt everything slide away into nothingness. I gave up. There was no fight in me left.

I died.

It turns out that dying isn't so bad. I felt that familiar feeling of home that I'd experienced in my childhood. However, not being ready to go is fucking traumatic as hell when you come back.

When I came to and realised I was alive, I wasn't the same. I lost my job with Dad. I needed support he couldn't offer. I couldn't sleep without seeing my life being stolen from me over and over again by those doctors. I developed PTSD. I became clinically depressed, anxious, mid-bi-polar and an insomniac.

Sleep was worse than dying. I'd wake up screaming and crying. So I'd pop another pill and try to get back to sleep. At around the same time my son was born, my little hero. He gave me purpose through that dark time, but it wasn't enough.

I injured my back trying to return to work. I was fueling myself with junk food, drugs, sex, medication, painkillers, cigarettes, everything and anything I could use to mask the physical and emotional pain. I gained weight, blowing up to 100kg from 74kg. I was dying; killing myself from the inside out.

So I started a business. Crazy right?! It turns out having something bigger to strive for was what I needed to heal. Shortly after starting up that business, my daughter was born, and similar to the life-altering moment in Thailand, the universe served me another spicy dish of, 'have you learned your lesson yet?'

I wasn't a healthy partner or father. I certainly wasn't the man I am today. My children's mother and I fell out. I found myself back at my mum's house. Alone. A fucking mess. I couldn't even call my children.

It was at that moment I realised a pattern. This is what happened more or less with my parents. I was repeating history. I cried. And I cried. And I cried. Until there were no tears left.

I had become the monster I'd vowed I'd never become. I was responsible for my pain and situation. I had to change. Then and there. This was a catalyst make-or-break moment.

So I did a fucking 180 that night. I owned my shit. I said sorry. And I started doing things differently. I began learning about self-awareness and personal development. Emotional intelligence. Mindfulness. Sexuality. Spirituality. Business. Marketing. Psychology. How to be a healthy father. How to listen and communicate with your partner and people in general. This shit wasn't taught to me as a kid or young adult. Where was the right of passage? The 'becoming a man' guidelines and support? I had to work it all out on my own.

Some magical shit happened on this journey of self-discovery. I found people that gave me the language to express myself healthily. I called in a tribe of people who knew that there's more to life than hustling, being angry, controlling women, hating your father, escaping and medicating.

I was able to let go of so much pain. I was able to heal and find myself. I accepted all parts of myself; the deeper I went on this journey, the healthier, happier and lighter I became!

I ended a 13-year relationship, sold my miserable cleaning business and travelled the world. I met an amazing new woman and redefined my purpose in life. I started a coaching business dedicated to helping others reinvent, rediscover and heal themselves. I became a better partner, father, businessman, and friend. A better human.

The more I stopped trying to fit in, the less I needed to run or hide. I stopped needing to escape or medicate. I didn't need to lash out or rage anymore. Being able to let go of this heavy, angry armour was painfully beautiful.

Underneath all this shit I had been carrying, was me.

The real me.

I reconnected myself to the universe and all its emotions. Plugged back in. Returned 'home'. Back to that feeling, like when I was a little boy. I forgave people. I apologised to people. Most importantly, I forgave myself.

I cried. I felt the decades of pain wash out of me. Like a real man, I felt the pain and let it go so I could keep moving forward. By discovering who I was, I healed who I had been.

When a man heals himself, all men heal, the world heals, and it becomes a safer place.

About the Author:

Richie Nelson is a Business and Mindset Mentor and father to two well-rounded little humans. He helps people slow down, clear emotional blocks and limiting beliefs, and realign their values so that they can transform their lives and reach their full potential without sacrificing what most matters to them (e.g. health, self, parenting, relationships, business, positive global change). Richie is on a mission to raise human consciousness and bring families closer together.

Connect with Richie:

Facebook:
www.facebook.com/richielukenelson
www.facebook.com/richierichkraft

Recommended Resources:

<u>Books:</u>

The Art of War - Lao Tzu
The Big Leap - Gay Hendricks
The One Thing - Gary Keller
The 5 Love Languages - Gary Chapman
Clear Your Shit - Dane Thomas
The Conscious Hustle - Dane Thomas
Extreme Ownership - Jocko Willink

<u>Websites:</u>

www.gottman.com/about/the-gottman-method
www.clearyyourshit.com
www.5lovelanguages.com/profile
Tai Lopez's 67 Steps : www.the67steps.com
Anything by Dr. John Demartini

Unmasking the Masculine
By Tim Vaughan

'When we hold out our hands to another man or take him in our arms to be held, he will most likely feel the father's hands he never held reaching through time and space.' ~ John Lee, At My Father's Wedding

I was eighteen. It was the night before leaving home to go to University. I felt a mixture of excitement and dread at the prospect of leaving: I desired the freedom and autonomy to be my own man yet still longed for the safety and warmth of being with my mum. Feeling confused, I sat with her as she lay in bed, a final mother and son moment before the big day. We were both churned up inside, so shared how we were feeling. I told her that I was worried about leaving her on her own, particularly as she and Dad had not long since separated. She told me not to worry, that she would be ok, but we both knew this was a lie.

She looked at me. I could see the love shining through the tears in her eyes as she said: 'You're a lovely sensitive man Tim. Don't lose that.'

And I promised. I reassured Mum that she had nothing to

worry about, that I wouldn't change, that I would always be the sensitive Tim that she knew.

As life unfolded, this promise was one that I neglected to keep.

My story is one of struggle. The struggle to be that man my mum saw. The struggle to feel safe enough to remove the many protective masks I adopted. The struggle to fully show up in relationships authentically, instead of denying my vulnerability and hiding the shadowy parts I didn't want others to see.

There is nothing exceptional or unusual about my story. It seems ordinary, such is the narrative around masculinity within our culture, which is why I want to share it because we *can* change the narrative. We *can* create a whole new dialogue. And we *can* shift the cultural paradigm of what it means to be a man.

I hope my story helps you to find the courage to look inside yourself, to face your shadow, your wounds, your shame and own *all* of you. I hope you find the bravery to express who you truly are to others, even if you don't quite fit the social expectations of masculinity. And I hope that my story – and indeed this book – triggers much needed, open and honest conversations with your sons, nephews, partners and friends about masculinity, and the importance of teaching our boys to express their needs and emotions.

My Story

After that moving conversation with my mum, I spent the best part of 25-years masking my sensitivity both in my relationships with women and my friendships with men. In truth, becoming a social chameleon had already begun in school. The desire to fit in and be accepted was so strong among boys at school; I was no different. More than anything I desperately wanted to be liked, believing that the only way was to be funny, act cool, pretend to be tough, and mask my vulnerability and emotions.

I've heard it said that there are only four emotions: sadness, joy, anger and fear. If this is true, then only two of these were permitted to us as boys in school. Anger was expressed freely, aggression a sure sign of masculinity, and joy readily accepted, especially if it was at the expense of someone else. Sadness and fear meanwhile were strictly off limits. Being secretly sensitive I was never very good at expressing anger, so joy became my default, which for me was about being funny, having a laugh and making light of things that I found emotionally painful. These unwritten codes were re-enforced regularly by other boys and me. We mocked, verbally abused and bullied anyone straying outside of these norms; I gave and received my fair share.

A good friend of mine suffered relentless abuse for crying

in the cinema at the end scene of E.T. I was there too, and I can still remember the huge lump in my throat, desperately trying to stop the tears coming. Despite this, I was one of the first to ridicule him, the perfect decoy for my own unexpressed emotions. Just imagine how different it might have been if we could have shared our emotion without fear of ridicule? No chance of that. Boys don't cry. The *ultimate* rule of masculinity.

The Man in the Mirror

I recall once saying to a friend after a Michael Jackson concert that I'd found his rendition of 'Man in the Mirror' really moving and that I'd *almost* cried (I *had* shed tears). Oh, what a mistake that was! The following day at school I was mocked with renditions of 'Man in the Mirror'. I was upset with my friend for telling others about my emotional moment, but of course, I denied it and laughed along with them, deflecting the ridicule and asserting my toughness by accusing my friend of crying too. Unbeknown to me at the time, this unconscious patterning became my survival strategy, and the protocol looked something like this:

Rule 1: Be funny. I have, after all, excelled at being funny. People like me because of this. So be funny. No matter what. Even at other people's expense.

I would learn to crave that feeling of being liked, even if it meant hurting others and me. It became an addictive pattern. But the pressure to be a fun guy would eventually take its toll in later life.

Rule 2: Be cool, stoic and aloof. The girls *love* it.

I genuinely believed this. The journals of my time at school are full of examples where I chose to play it cool rather than express how I felt about a girl I liked. I still read them now and want to scream out, 'Tell her how you feel!'

Rule 3: Pretend to be hard and tough. Turn your pain onto someone else. Even though this goes against *everything* you know to be true of Sensitive Tim.

The tough-guy act wasn't sustainable; being beaten up in a fight made sure of that.

Rule 4: Do not cry or show *any* weakness or vulnerability to your friends. Cling to this rule for dear life. Never forget the 'Man in the Mirror'!

This unconscious pattern of behaviours, or survival strategy, followed me into adulthood and the minefield of romantic relationships. *Be funny. Be cool. Don't show vulnerability. You'll be fine.* As you can imagine, this wasn't a recipe for lasting love.

No More Mr Nice Guy

From some of my early encounters in the world of romance, a message I repeatedly heard from men, women and the media was, 'Nice guys don't get anything'. 'You're a nice guy but...' was a phrase I often heard as I experienced another rejection. *What's the matter with me? I need to get an edge, be cooler, and then they'll like me,* I thought.

Excessive partying and drinking became my edge in a life hidden away from my family. Shame stopped me from letting them know about *this* Tim. The Manchester music and clubbing scene were alive and kicking, I had loads of friends and was engaging in lots of casual sex, which was giving me some short-lived sense of purpose. My whole self-worth was wrapped up in being popular and 'successful' with women. A new identity formed. A new mask. No more Mr Nice Guy. Party Tim was in town, and I liked him, and other people seemed to like him too.

Among groups of men, I became fiercely competitive over girls. I hated it if they were more successful with women than me and I began to see girls as conquests, notches on the bedpost. I'd freely swap sordid tales of my conquests and revelled in what I believed was the admiration of my friends. They would laugh at my stories, and I took this as encouragement. I'd happily swoop in on a girl that a friend liked, a desperate attempt to prove my worthiness and masculinity to other men. On a couple of occasions friends called-out my behaviour, yet I'd shrug it off and tell them to 'get over it'. Deep down I knew they were right. It troubled me that I had upset them, but I couldn't let them know, couldn't show that kind of weakness. *Stick to the survival strategy, Tim.* And so I did. I continued with the bravado, a facade of joviality and banter yet feeling crushed on the inside.

I began to dislike the way I was behaving and the person I was becoming, but my ego was out of control, driven by an insatiable need for the approval of others. When I was with my family, I'd go back to the kind, sensitive Tim that they knew. With anyone else, I'd wear the appropriate mask depending on my environment. Throughout my twenties, I genuinely thought this was enough for me. I could handle it. I was happy *most* of the time.

When Cracks Start to Show

Into my thirties, I became increasingly unhappy with living this party lifestyle, but it was such a slow creep of dissatisfaction that I never felt inclined to do anything about it. I knew I wanted to have a family - I loved kids – but every relationship turned sour. *They always leave me, what's wrong with me? What's wrong with them? I'm not meeting the right kind of girls.* These were the thoughts I'd have. Initially, I had been drawn to girls who I saw as funny, cool, and beautiful, a mirror of what I was presenting to the world. Given the social circles I was hanging around in, they tended to be into partying in a big way too, so hardly the settling down type. I was craving a relationship with real depth but didn't know how to go about it. When I wasn't partying, I was recovering from the excess of the night before. My emotions were so up and down because of this that it was difficult to trust my feelings.

People liked being around me. I was popular and used to revel in being the centre of attention and being the party animal who stayed up all night. I was addicted to the reassuring feeling that I was loved by many. It mattered to me to have a lot of friends. The downside of this was that I used to feel such pressure to perform the role of the outgoing, funny guy. The clown mask was becoming well and truly stuck to my face, but it was beginning to show cracks. To the people in my social circle I was happy-go-lucky, always smiling, but it was like I was living someone else's life. Towards the latter end of my partying days, I even went as far as creating an alter-ego for myself at festivals: Rainbowface. Everyone loved Rainbowface. *I* loved Rainbowface. He was an expression of me, the parts that I wanted people to see and love. Covered in face paint, I literally wore a mask to keep up the pretence that this life I was living was enough and I was happy. Behind the mask was a man who was becoming increasingly sad, lonely and lost.

I remember being at a club one night in my late thirties, following a heart-breaking relationship split. I was surrounded by people dancing and having a great time. Dancing was the last thing I felt like doing. I just wanted to sit and talk with someone about how sad and lost I was feeling. *How did this happen? How had I become this person who is so conditioned to be an extrovert? I don't want to belong to this tribe anymore but how do I leave when all my friendship groups and sense of identity are caught up in it? What happened to the kind, sensitive, gentle man who had sat on his mum's bed all those years ago?*

I stopped still on the edge of the dancefloor, and I started to feel an immense heaviness in my chest. I felt sad, tears streaming down my face. I made a sharp exit so that nobody could see and walked into the dark, wet Manchester night alone. The tears didn't stop all night and all the next day. I began to think I might be having an emotional breakdown as the tears just kept coming. I never spoke of any of these feelings to my friends or partners. How frightening it can be to remove the mask that had served me so well for so long. *Who would I be if I wasn't this crazy, party-loving, sociable guy? Would people like me?* All my life I'd so desperately wanted to be liked – loved - that I'd become who I thought people wanted me to be. I had no real idea of who I was anymore. Lost and alone in what felt like a wasteland.

The partying and drinking eventually stopped, but my relationship difficulties continued.

Removing the Mask

In relationships I'd learned to become very passive, seeing to my partner's needs while not knowing how to express my own. Instead, my insecurities, increasing anger and longing for a deep connection grew. Sadly, I took this increasing sense of dis-ease into my marriage. It lasted nearly three years. We broke up, but not before we brought the most incredible gift, our daughter, into the world. What a joy she is and how amazing it is to be a father. Sadly, having a child wasn't enough to save our marriage.

It took the birth of my daughter, the death of a close friend and (soon afterwards) the break-up of my marriage for me to take stock of my life. I felt deep shame that my marriage had broken down so quickly. All the people that had come to the wedding to wish us on our way with love - what would they think? I was so desperately sad that we couldn't find a way through the difficulties, heartbroken at being separated from my daughter. This was my rock bottom.

I needed some head-space, so I decided to go on a week-long retreat abroad, which proved to be a real turning point in my life. For the first time, I sat with my sadness. I'd spent so long running away from this feeling. The tears flowed, but unlike before I didn't hide them away. For the first time in my life, I allowed others to see me at my most vulnerable. I realised that I had never felt safe enough to show my vulnerability in relationships with women and friendships with men. I'd been afraid of being seen as weak in some way, and not coping. That week, surrounded by love and the acceptance of others, the healing and rebuilding process began.

A lovely lady gave me a letter on the last day of the retreat. It was beautiful. It was reminding me to continue to show my gentleness and kindness. That it *is* ok to be a 'Gentleman'. It gave me the confidence to be open-hearted, to share my vulnerability and to express what I wanted and needed from a relationship. I began to come to life again and communicate from my heart. I was starting to become the man I had always wanted to be, that I always was deep inside. Kind, fun-loving, considerate, sensitive and open-hearted.

Soon afterwards Suzie walked into my life. We met at a festival, and I can remember talking to her so freely about my experiences on the retreat and about my life. It felt incredibly freeing to be able to speak from my heart without a filter and fear. I felt the most congruent I had ever felt. The very first date we had I completely broke down about the death of my friend. Until then I hadn't allowed myself to grieve for him. I couldn't believe how vulnerable I was with her. I will never forget how she emotionally held me that evening. The next day I experienced a vulnerability hangover for revealing so much so soon and for crying. Without prompting she sent through a film by Brené Brown about shame. In it Brené talks of how men can feel great shame around showing vulnerability. This made so much sense to me. She goes on to describe how some women are not comfortable seeing their men in such a vulnerable state. Thankfully Suzie was.

Conscious Loving

It seems to me that both men and women's perspective on what it means to be a man is heavily skewed by a society where men hold power and women are largely excluded from it. Men are meant to be strong and not show emotions that 'weaken' them. A few weeks later I revealed to Suzie all that happened in my life. I hid nothing from her. I was so afraid of her judgment and of losing her; the opposite was true. It brought us closer together and enabled her to open up about the things that evoked shame in her. It was extraordinary to me that somehow revealing the worst of myself acted as a catalyst for the depth of connection I had always craved.

Fast forward two years and Suzie and I are still together in a consciously co-committed relationship. Through the 'Conscious Loving' work of Gaye and Katie Hendricks, we've both spent a lot of time finding a way to communicate when our insecurities and shadows are showing up. It is about showing up for each other with absolute honesty, openness and personal responsibility for our own emotions. It's a practice and a discipline. At times it's exhausting but always worth it as our understanding and love of each other deepens. We are finding a way to communicate our emotional needs, often hidden behind the more obvious anger and upset at not getting those needs met. What joy and freedom there is in being in a relationship where we are both fully seen, heard, respected and loved!

Over the past two years, my life has completely turned around for the better. My relationships are richer and deeper, and I'm showing up in the world with so much more courage to be vulnerable and open-hearted. When we show our vulnerability to others, it allows them to share in our humanity and connect at a deeper level. I know that Suzie was pivotal and entered my life at just the right time, but she was not the reason I found my way out of the wasteland. It was my willingness to take full responsibility for what had happened in my life and to get help from others to support me in shedding light on my destructive patterns of behaviour. Without doing this, it is entirely probable that Suzie would not be in my life right now.

As I look back on my partying days, I do have some great memories. But it's painful to acknowledge that I spent twenty-five years unconsciously committed to staying on the surface and hiding behind many masks. *If I'm funny, people will love me. If I show I'm intelligent, crazy, extrovert, the party guy, people will love me.* Because people wouldn't love a sensitive, kind, 'nice guy', right? Well, you bet they do!

Doing 'Men's Work'

I'm not always Sensitive Tim, even today. Sometimes I'm angry, insensitive, moody, mistrusting, judgemental, scattered and insecure. This shadow part of myself is always around and does get triggered, no more so than when in the company of men. I have often complained to Suzie that I wanted to connect with male friends deeply, beyond the usual banter and competitiveness. So I joined a men's circle.

A men's circle is a group of men committed to supporting each other's healing and personal growth. The circle provides a safe and supportive place for men to consciously meet in community in a unique way outside of many of the usual ways men get together. These are growing in number, and I believe they play a vital role in helping men to feel safe enough to express their emotions among other men. Through working with this group and the Mankind Project, I have been able to explore the concept of masculinity, acknowledging the need to be gentle and sensitive but also to value authentic masculine power. As a result, I have learned to be much stronger with my boundaries, I have healthier ways of expressing anger, and I have a clear sense of purpose now. The men in these groups impress me greatly. They are good open-hearted men, and I am so pleased to be joining them in the work they are doing in the world.

This 'men's work', as it is known, has helped me get to the crux of why I always felt like I wasn't enough. I connected to my deepest wound, my relationship with my father, or lack of it as a child. Through a powerful physiological and emotional process, I had the opportunity to express my childhood and adult rage fully. I was longing for my father to spend time with me, to be seen, and held physically and emotionally by him. But my father was emotionally unavailable, so, like many boys, I learnt through his detachment that I wasn't enough.

I'd never felt emotionally safe with my dad as a child. He didn't know how to play or connect with us emotionally. It wasn't until he was nearly sixty-one that he was diagnosed as having a mild form of Asperger Syndrome (the higher functioning end of Autistic Spectrum Disorder). My dad and I have resolved our differences over the years and have become extremely close. He's a good man, himself the son of a father who had also been emotionally distant. Over the past year, we have been talking about his life in a series of conversations. At times this has been beautiful, and at times extremely moving and upsetting. I have asked some challenging questions. He always answered them truthfully and thoughtfully. By doing this, he allowed me to walk in his shoes and come to understand him fully. Holding nothing back, he shared with me the most vulnerable parts of him and all his humanity. This proved to be a wonderful healing gift for us both.

I can see now how my insecurity has played out in all my relationships. Through this work, I've realised that I have never felt safe enough to be open with *any* man. As a result, I've never provided safety for them to open fully to me. And there was *me* complaining about not having deep friendships with male friends. It's been a real joy to be able to speak from the heart with some of my old friends about this, and I've been surprised at their openness to share their vulnerabilities. All it takes is one person to start the conversation.

Perhaps the most profound moment in my personal development journey was a recent experience at an Authentic Relating workshop. During it, I became aware that one man was powerfully triggering my shadow side. For some reason I mistrusted him, and I felt myself becoming competitive with him. Old familiar feelings were stirring again. Ordinarily, I would have stayed away from him, but this time I decided to walk towards these feelings and get curious about them. I decided to tell this man how I was feeling and asked if he would help me to work through this. I knew that this was my stuff and was not about him. Thankfully, he didn't take offence and agreed to help me work through what was happening. What occurred throughout the next hour was mind-blowing. Initially, we discussed paying attention to the feelings that had been arising. Albeit helpful, there was more to do. Working from intuition, he asked: 'What would it be like if I held you in some way?' I thought it unusual, but I was open to trying.

I found it extremely difficult at first to allow myself to be held by another man, but eventually, he was supporting my full weight by holding me under my arms from behind. At that point, he placed his hand on my forehead and held it there. What happened next was a huge emotional outpouring of grief from me. I was uncontrollably sobbing my heart out. *What was going on?* In those moments I was getting a multitude of insights. I realised that this was how I had longed to be held emotionally and physically by my father. It was the most powerfully healing experience I have ever had in my life. I still find it astonishing that I shared this deeply moving and healing experience with the very man I had treated with such suspicion, the man who had triggered my darker emotions. I am so grateful to him for being completely in service to me. It would have been easy for him to have dismissed me and walked away.

The notion of men touching is a delicate subject, almost taboo. Most of us have been taught not to touch each other affectionately. We have generally figured out alternatives like sports, fist pumps, body checks, good-natured jostling, dead arms and back slaps. Hugging has become more acceptable in recent times, though often accompanied with back-slapping. Unfortunately, these don't work when a man is feeling sad and may need a more gentle, supportive touch. What my experience taught me is that affection and intimacy have very little to do with sexuality. It was a profoundly healing experience. What if we as men could turn to our brothers and ask for help and healing? In this way, our relationships, friendships, places of work and the world could become a safer place to be. This capacity for men to trust each other and heal each other's wounds is what the world needs if we are to heal the male psyche.

Of all the personal development work I have done, the most transformational has been with other men. I cannot recommend the empowering work of the *Mankind Project* enough to any man. It strikes me that many men go to their womenfolk for healing and deep connection. I've experienced men holding emotional space for each other, and it is different. Not better or worse, just different. When men come together and feel safe with one another, the world becomes a safer place.

'There is much about our experience as men that can only be shared with, and understood by, other men. There are stories we can tell only to those who have wrestled in the dark with the same demons and been wounded by the same angels. Only men understand the secret fears that go with the territory of masculinity.' ~ Sam Keen, Fire in the Belly

I sit here now as a 46-year-old man just beginning to understand who I really am and what it means to be a good man in this world. Sorting out my inner-world has been a painful process but one worth going through. The rewards are great. It has helped me deal with a lot of suppressed anger and sadness that I was wrapped up in. It has led to a deeper understanding of my inner-world. There's more work to be done, but now that I am more closely connected and comfortable on the inside, I have more presence and emotional availability for others. This 'inner weeding' has allowed me to clear space for more joy in life. I've learned that there is great strength in showing vulnerability and in revealing my shame; it's the route to deeper connection. I now know that a man doesn't have to live up to any narrow, societal image of manhood. I've come home after many years in the wasteland. I feel congruent and grounded in who I am, leading from my heart and encouraging other men to do the same. My wonderful array of masks that I've worn adorn the crumbling walls around my heart. They're still there to be used now and again, but I noticed the other day that they're getting quite dusty.

Reader Notes:

Use these questions to explore your masculinity.

- ❖ What does masculinity mean to you? How has your definition of masculinity shaped your behaviours and experiences throughout your life?
- ❖ What are some of the masks that you wear in different social situations? Who is the most authentic version of you beneath the mask(s)?
- ❖ Explore your own unmet and unexpressed needs from childhood to now. How have they impacted your life? In what ways do they manifest in your behaviour? How can YOU meet your own needs?

About the Author:

Tim is a freelance trainer, facilitator, coach and writer. He works with a learning and development company, with whom he encourages leaders in organisations to become more of who they are when leading others. He challenges them to lead from their heart and to share their vulnerability and humanity with their teams. By doing so, they can create emotionally safe places for other people to be creative and to develop.

He is currently working on developing a series of workshops for men and on-line men's circles to enable men to know and embody healthy adult masculinity. His vision is to create safe spaces (face to face and online) for men to come together in brotherhood, connect deeply, and learn to trust and support each other. If you feel the call, then connect with Tim.

Connect with Tim:

Facebook: facebook.com/tim.vaughan.7777
Email: timvaughan@outlook.com

Recommended Resources:

<u>Websites:</u>

www.mankindprojectuki.org
www.learningtoinspire.co.uk
www.ted.com/talks/brene_brown_listening_to_shame
www.ted.com/talks/brene_brown_on_vulnerability
www.hendricks.com

<u>Books:</u>

Iron John – Robert Bly
Conscious Loving – Gaye and Katie Hendricks
A Circle of Men – Bill Kauth
At My Father's Wedding – John Lee

King, Warrior, Magician, Lover – Robert Moore

Fire in the Belly – Sam Keen

Screaming on the Inside
By Tom Jordan

'We are people, individuals comprising a variety of sexes, races, shifting sexualities and all the rest of it. Every convention that tries to reinforce this difference is a step back. Notions of gender pointlessly separate men from women, but also mothers from daughters and fathers from sons.' ~ Robert Webb

'So, are you gay?'

'I'm sorry?'

'Are you gay?'

That was the question posed to me aged ten. I didn't play 'kiss chase'. I don't know why. I'd like to pretend that it was out of some pre-adolescent, naturally developed sense of feminism. In reality, I was frightened of intimacy, of displays of affection. Maybe that's another subject for a different time.

Kiss Chase. Well, that's a negative fucking life lesson right there. Boys chase girls to steal kisses. Yes, *steal* kisses. That's the game. Physically pursue the girls until they are corned, at which point they are *obliged* no less to allow you, the boy, to enact a light-hearted physical assault.

For no reason other than my self-interested neuroses I didn't want to take part. So this led my friends to question my sexuality. I had already had a hetero-normative identity beaten into me by the world around me, so for anyone to suggest that I might be anything other than straight must be a bad thing.

Being gay is bad. Being anything than straight is bad. It's not safe to be anything else. Yes, that's the very clear message I learned aged ten.

Now, in my thirties, I'm generally too scared to tell anyone that I'm bisexual. It shouldn't be relevant. And I don't want to make it a focal point of this chapter. I'm just like you. Whether you're straight, gay, bi, queer, pan, trans, asexual (sorry if I've left anyone out). Or maybe I'm *not* the same. Does it matter? My heart still beats. I still bleed. I still feel pain and love. And hate, as much as I tell myself I don't. My internal instinct is to tell you: 'Yeah, I'm bi, but I could still kick the shit out of you'. But I'd be lying, not only to you but myself. I've never been in a fight in my life. Not a real one, though I did get beaten up once.

Everything makes us question our masculinity. Our physical and mental health, our place in society, our wealth (or lack of), the list goes on. The truth is, people have a shit time. Not all the time, but everyone does. And my story is no different. It meanders. And in this chapter, it drifts between my memories and my current innermost thoughts as I write. Because this shit *is* real. And this bullshit machismo culture has a lot to answer for.

The Diary of a Lost Identity

I'm 17 and lying on the floor of my bedroom. I feel more grounded on the floor; it embraces me and my depression. I'm feeling low physically as well as mentally. I cry. Frequently. My mind is a clouded, frustrated, broken mess. I can't tell you how I got here. I don't understand myself, only know how I'm expected to behave. I'm supposed to be strong, productive, confident, tough, fit, straight, smart, independent, sporty, slim, dominating, arrogant, a rugby player, an academic, better than my peers. And while I'm some of these things, I'm also sensitive, emotionally unstable, an underachiever, a daydreamer, a procrastinator, a creative, bisexual, crap at sports, unfit, and have low self-esteem.

Be more muscular. Have more sexual partners. Don't cry, my inner voice screams at me, daily.

Age 21

I'm a binge-drinking, binge-smoking, binge-eating, binge-spending wreck. I'm anxious and obsess over different negative thoughts. I count things internally with no control. I hate myself. I've developed the arrogance, but it's only produced a greater sense of self-loathing. I make poor decisions and then feel ashamed.

I'm a fight choreographer. I know. Seriously? Yes, it's a real job. And it's a part of the theatre industry. So it's much less interested in machismo and far more concerned with equality and honesty and vulnerability. Is it fuck. It's just another pissing contest. And a great way to pretend to be macho without actually having to be.

'So you'd be pretty hardcore in a fight right? You know, if someone started a fight with you on the street?'

Violence repulses me. I hate it, and it scares me. It's part of why I study it and work to present it to an audience in a safe environment. There's too much ego in the world. Too much shouting and bravado. Too much 'manning up'. It makes my head hurt. Wouldn't it be lovely if we could all just be ourselves?

Age 26

Where is my life going? What is wrong with me? I'm pathetic and in constant turmoil. I am selfish and full of self-entitlement. I'm a coward, and I doubt everything. The simplest action - sending an email, making a phone call - takes several weeks. I'm opinionated and thoughtless. I feel like I'm comfortable in myself, but at the same time, I feel like a fraud. I talk the talk but rarely do I walk the walk. Still, I cry. Still, I loathe myself.

I'm doing a physical job this week. I've just taken the pack of plasters (band-aids) from my toddler to cover my blisters. Blisters that I developed on my hands after one morning of manual labour. I almost said: 'No! Daddy needs those because he's a fanny!'

What? Blisters are what human beings get when they experience friction at points in their body where repetitive force is not normally applied. Why is that something to feel embarrassed about? How does it connect to a scale of masculinity and why does it require an internal, prejudiced slight against whatever demographic the needless word 'fanny' (aka vagina) is supposed to apply to?

Age 28

I'm falling apart. I don't recognise myself. I've beaten my identity out of myself.

The fear. Of what other people think. Am I strong enough? Am I masculine enough?

Age 29

My life changes. I'm single. I start to look at myself. I meet a truly wonderful woman. She's intelligent, funny, and has a sparkle in her eyes.

Boys. Chase girls. To steal kisses.

Age 30

We're married now. Our first child is on her way. I lead a double life. Everything is incredible, but I'm starting to take my wife with me. I mean well, but I'm selfish. I indulge my worries and fears at the expense of hers. We share our life. We have fun; we go on adventures. Our first daughter is born, and she is everything.

Still my mind rots. That's because I control my mind, me alone, and I don't know what I'm doing. The brain is a complex, vibrant, emotional machine and I'm ignorant. Incompetent. I'm wrapped up in myself while professing to put my family first. We don't realise it yet, but I'm damaging my wife's sense of self as well as my own. We argue, not a lot, but when we do, it's explosive. I'm self-absorbed, so the disputes always go further than they should. Sometimes I can even see myself causing damage with my actions. I'm not aware of it consciously yet, but all that pressure, all the expectation, I'd put on myself. I am self-important and entitled. It is ugly.

Fuck, I'm writing this and struggling to not sound like a poor privileged white, middle-class male. I loathe half of what I've written. If I'm bold in my writing, I look back and cringe at my confidence. If I meander and lack conviction, I baulk at my weakness. I've been taught to be bold and dominating, and that sensitivity is bad. So I'm like a dove with half a wing flying round in circles. Or no, wait, not a dove. A hawk. No, an eagle. No a fucking griffon. Oh, who gives a shit. My head is screaming.

Don't pity me. Society gives me everything. Just don't be like me.

Age 32

Our second child is on her way. My wife is ill. Seriously ill. The pregnancy is taking its toll on her physical health. Complications mean that we nearly lose her and our baby. My wife keeps going, no matter what happens. I care for her, but I'm floundering.

She survives. Most of her. There is damage to her system, but she's alive. Our baby is alive. The relief is immense.

It's the end of the year. I'm unbearable. I'm anxious and obsessed. I upset my wife frequently. My children don't deserve this. It would be better if I were dead. That's what I think frequently.

I wear nail polish. Not all the time. Sometimes it's green. Sometimes it's a kind of iridescent purple.

'I can't take you seriously with your nails painted.'

'Did your little girl do that?'

No. I did. Because I like it and it's an expression of me. And I've spent too much time agonising over something as seemingly innocuous as nail varnish to give a shit what people think anymore.

Age 33

I've been waiting for counselling on the NHS for some time. My wife is stronger than I am and she supports me with the energy she can't spare. After unforeseen, uncontrollable issues with our industries, we are also struggling financially. I stutter when I am stressed. The tension in my body is such that I shake when I can't cope. Life is not without joy, but I find only extremes.

My first CBT (Cognitive Behavioural Therapy) session arrives, and I'm terrified. What if it doesn't work for me? What then? What will she do? How will she cope with me? My counsellor breaks things down for me. He explains how we're going to work and he talks to me about tackling the root of my mental health problem through therapy. There is hope. I breathe. I smile.

I have spent many hours feeling down about my chin. It's the main reason I have a beard. My chin is weak, not strong how I'd expect a manly chin to be. One of the only parts of my body that I can do nothing about. If you see my beardless chin, I feel ashamed. If my shirt is off, I feel ashamed. If I'm awake and breathing, I likely feel ashamed. Ashamed of my lack of muscle, of my self-doubt, of my voice or my hair length or the clothes I'm wearing. The cacophony of the masculine ideal is unbearable.

Age 33 ½

It's been some weeks. I'm noticeably calmer. I feel more in control. I listen more. I put things in perspective.

I. Put. Things. In. Perspective.

I am more productive. I do more. I care less about the things that don't matter and more about the things that do. I am kinder and more thoughtful. It's a long road, but there is hope.

Boys. Don't. Cry.

A New Chapter

And here I am, back in the present. I still make mistakes and lots of them, but I have strategies now. I still worry. I still overreact. I take steps backwards, but I now take forward steps too. I have more time for others. My body is more relaxed. I upset my wife still, but now it's largely forgivable stuff. I feel like I'm a good father. I mean, sometimes I don't, but on the whole, I do. I'm not perfect, and that's ok. I didn't know how hard women had it, how hard other people had it. I thought I did. Now I'm listening. Now I'm learning. It's the tip of the iceberg, but I am developing, growing even.

I don't want others to face the mental health issues that I

have, to be trapped in the chaos of their mind and hiding their true self from the world.

I want to wear nail polish. I do it. People question it. People comment, and rarely negatively. I can see that it gives others courage too.

'Everyone's different. We've all got our own stuff going on.'

'Yeah, I know what you mean. I'm normally too scared to tell anyone, but I'm bi.'

'That's cool dude. I'm glad you felt able to tell me.'

So here it is, my chapter, my life. But this chapter isn't about sexuality. It's about authenticity. I'm not about sexuality, but I'm not straight, and that's ok. It doesn't have to hurt. It doesn't have to be something that I hide. It can be something to be proud of, one of the multifaceted expressions of me. Something that my wife and my friends stand by me knowing, while still seeing me as the same person, albeit a little braver.

It feels good to share. Maybe it'll show someone else that it's ok to be you, the true you beneath the mask and armour that you wear. Give yourself a break. Whoever you are, whatever is going on in your life, be who you are. Respect who you are. Be proud of who you are.

And if you need to, cry. Not conforming to society's masculine ideology does not make you any less of a man.

About the Author:

Tom is a theatre creative based near Brighton. He is married to an incredible woman, Danielle, and together they are parents to a pair of bright, adventurous little girls. Tom works as a director, fight director, writer and actor (occasionally). He grew up in Gloucestershire and is an avid collector of hobbies – board games, drawing, playing musical instruments to name a few – though nothing is as rock n roll as his pencil collection. Tom attended an all boys grammar school, before studying film and theatre at the University of Reading. He completed an apprenticeship as a stage combat instructor in 2009 and currently works across the UK. He loves living by the sea, exploring European cities and discovering exciting foods. Whilst he loves adventuring and being in the rehearsal room alike, he is never happier than when he's in the company of his three favourite ladies.

The Mask
By Mark Newey

'Be who you are, say what you feel, because those who mind don't matter and those who matter don't mind.' ~ Dr. Seuss

I'm a good boy. I do everything I'm told. I grow into a stable, confident, out-going, man's man. I do the banter, the back-slapping, the slightly risqué jokes, especially about women.

At least, I *did*.

I spent the first 40 years of my life wearing a mask and being somebody else. Beneath the bravado, I felt weak, insecure, frightened and not a *real* man. But of course, I could never admit that to myself. Above all, I carried a deep sense of shame.

Then my life came crashing down around me.

A breakdown allowed me to find out who I really am - of course, who I always was: a gentle, empathetic man who's entirely in touch with his feminine side, and proud of it.

I'm now confident and strong, without the need for a facade. I connect with and relate to people in a deeper, more meaningful way. I'm content and make a positive difference in the lives of others. The persona of my earlier years has been well-and-truly left behind while the gentle, modest and inclusive charisma of my true self has blossomed.

So what happened?

In the Beginning

I was born with very severe asthma, spending the first year of life in and out of the hospital with a 50/50 chance of survival. Naturally, I don't remember that time, but I now see that even then my inner strength pulled me through.

I was sent to boarding school aged seven and got bullied. Boarding school is undoubtedly a privilege, but it's not always a happy one! The prefect in my dormitory would pour water on me every night, presumably because I was snoring and wheezing, so I didn't get a decent night's sleep for months.

I spent two terms in absolute misery and shame, living as the pathetic human being I believed myself to be. At Christmas, I burst into floods of tears and admitted everything to my parents; the shame deepened.

All the cool guys were in the sports teams, especially rugby, but I didn't stand a chance. A part of me knew I could have been in all of the teams, I was more than capable, yet I couldn't run more than a short distance without gasping for breath.

Then a miracle happened. Aged 12, my asthma vanished. I got into the 1st Xv rugby team and 1st X1 football team and ran the swimming team in the summer. The other boys, in awe of this transformation, suddenly welcomed me with open arms.

So this is who I became: the macho, bantery, arrogant and cool sporting hero. Finally, I'd made it! 'Mark The Man' had found his feet at last.

'Mark The Man'

I went off to public school and, despite the surface confidence, the shame came with me. I kept pushing it down and bouncing back with exaggerated pride. Nevertheless, I thrived. I was in all of the sports teams, reasonably bright and was a pretty good role model for the younger lads coming into the boarding house behind me.

When I look back, I realise the empathetic part of me was there all those years ago. I used to spend time with the younger boys who were often home-sick or struggling with the macho environment. As a result of this combination of projected confidence and subtle empathy, I was elected Head of House in my final year, which brought with it all sorts of privileges, including being allowed to go to the pub.

Then disaster struck! I got caught smoking and was demoted. The shame washed over me like a flood. I'd let everybody down: the headmaster, my housemaster, my parents, my brother (who was in the same house), and most importantly, the boys in the house to whom I was a role model.

Despite being reinstated the following term, I felt half 'the man' I was three months previously.

Without thinking about what I really wanted out of life or indeed who I was, I went to university in complete confusion. I knew I had to stand up and be 'the man', but my inner strength had deserted me. I felt weak, pathetic and a failure. I did my best to put the macho mask on; after all, that's what you do!

During Freshers' Week, I went to sign up for the rugby club. My whole identity and measure of manliness were attached to being on the rugby team. However, when I went to enrol, the 1st team captain was sat there, heavily intoxicated and eating none other than a wine glass. That threw me completely. How bloody stupid! What a complete twat! At that moment, I knew it wasn't for me and walked away. That was the very first time I questioned what it meant to be a *real* man. Whatever the truth, I knew eating wine glasses wasn't it.

I signed up with Moseley, an excellent local club and eventually made the 2nds. I was happy with that: there was an England player in the 1sts, and I knew I wasn't that good. There was no question that while the play on the pitch was aggressive, physical and macho, the guys erred on the gentlemanly side (although less so after 12 or 13 pints of beer on a Saturday night after the game).

But even then in my early twenties, there was one part of rugby life I disliked: the banter in the showers. A lot of the guys would ridicule their girlfriends in their absence, often with quite explicit detail, and only spoke of women in a derogatory, objectifying way. I realised later that they were quite decent guys, but many of them felt inadequate as men and struggled to live with society's expectations of them. One of their ways of dealing with this was to band together and speak disrespectfully of women. I hated it. But I never really questioned myself as to why. I just went along with the banter.

Playing rugby at a high level helped me regain my sense of manhood and my confidence. I left university with a 2:1 and six job offers. Life was looking good. 'Mark The Man' was back!

Living the Dream

Fast forward 15 years, and I had it all: a beautiful family, a lovely house in a 'picture box' village, a top of the range BMW, and I was globetrotting for work. I was living the dream. I had everything.

At least, from the outside, it looked that way.

Deep down there was a nagging doubt, but I wasn't going to let it surface. I carried on, bulldozing my way through any problem that arose. But gradually two things started to grind me down.

The obvious one was the workload and lifestyle. Typically I would fly out at 3 pm on Sunday afternoon and return home exhausted by 10 pm Friday night. I would then go into the office on Saturday for several hours to clear my in-tray (no laptops and e-mails in those days!).

Not surprisingly this started to take its toll. But part of me knew there was something else going on. It is only with hindsight, having discovered my highest value is respect, I realised that the macho corporate culture was slowly killing me. I didn't apprehend how toxic the 'dog-eat-dog' environment was: it was normal to respect absolutely nobody, except for your boss who expected nothing less. And my last corporate boss was an utter bastard; he even demanded that I go to the office the day the removal vans were delivering our worldly goods to our new home.

It was normal to stab people in the back, trample over your weaker colleagues and generally not give a shit about anyone. Again with hindsight, the real me was starting to poke through. I began to struggle with the office politics and the necessity of 'licking the boots' of the senior directors, especially given I had zero respect for them.

Having given several years of blood, sweat and tears, I was then made redundant six months after relocating my family to be nearer the office; the manner in which it was done would undoubtedly cakewalk a constructive dismissal case in today's world. But that was typical of my American employers. They were planning to sell the company and so were callously stripping back overheads to maximise profitability: they'd already planned to dismiss me long before I uprooted a hundred miles from friends and family.

I applied for other jobs but it was when the economy was in tatters in the late '80's, and after several months I realised I was going to have to set up my own business. After several iterations, the company took off and it looked like being made redundant was the best thing that could have happened. But also, having wobbled on the manhood front for a year or two, 'Mark The Man' was back again.

As the business grew, I took on a business partner who was

a bulldog from the City, and we took on 15 employees with all of the overheads that came with it. Life was good. Diamond necklace for the wife, expensive designer watch for me, and public school for the kids. I was living the high-life. What more could I want?

The Collapse

One day we walked into the office to discover a fax from our biggest corporate client pulling our contract - 70% of our business - with no notice. Over the next three months, my company and eight other fellow suppliers went bust. I negotiated with suppliers and helped my staff get new jobs where possible.

My partner went to the States and left me to clean up the mess. A few weeks later, I could no longer take the strain: I physically collapsed.

I didn't know what had hit me. One day I was functioning, the next I was on the floor, sobbing. The next couple of months went by in a fog. I rarely left the house and some days didn't even leave the bedroom.

One day, my then 4-year-old daughter scrambled onto my bed and said: 'I miss you, Daddy.' After she'd gone, I thought to myself, *what are you talking about my beautiful baby? I haven't left the house for months.* It took a while, but then it hit me: I was only there in body, not in mind or spirit!

This was the catalyst I needed to get back on my feet. But that's when the shame hit again, and this time it was a tsunami, not a flood. 'Mark the Man' was broken. I spent months trying to come back but was so lonely. My incredible wife had in the meantime stood up, got a job and held the family together. But that was *my* job, so this merely exacerbated the shame. When things were terrible, I ate supper on my own in another room: I couldn't bear to be with my wife and my three girls. I felt completely emasculated. I'd failed them. What was the point in being there? They didn't need me. I had no purpose. My wife genuinely didn't have much time to care for me; she was too busy holding the family together. I was on my own, spiralling into some very dark thinking.

Turning My Wounds into my Work

Eventually, that core inner strength that kept me alive aged one began to re-assert itself. I wanted to know how I was creating the mess in my head, so I started to read books on how the mind works. The more I read, the more fascinated I became and the more I healed. After a while, I realised that this was my purpose: this is why I'm here. I picked myself up and over the next three years trained in neuroscience and set up a psychotherapy practice, specialising in stress, anxiety and depression.

I work by teaching my clients how their mind works: how they create their reality including the reality they *don't* want. We then dive deep to find out who they *really* are, not whom they feel they should be. We then work on unpacking the unconscious programmes and beliefs that are holding them back and start to put together a new life vision allowing them to step into their real selves.

Having spent 18 months in counselling myself, I knew my modality had to be different. Indeed 65% of my clients have already been to counselling and CBT before they come to see me. Over the last 18 years, I've since helped nearly 3,000 people overcome – not manage or medicate - these debilitating mental health issues.

Manhood Shame

Over the years my male client base has soared, typically falling into two categories: the burnt-out corporate executives and entrepreneurs, and millennials/Gen Z's (16-26-year-olds). It took me a while, but I discovered a common thread running through many, if not most, of those clients: Manhood Shame. A theme I know well.

Manhood Shame is failure. At work. At school. At university. On the rugby field. In your marriage. With money. With your children. With your friends.

Manhood Shame is being wrong. Defective. Weak. Too

soft. Not 'manly' enough.

Manhood Shame is showing fear, admitting that you're scared, being vulnerable.

Manhood Shame is showing emotions. Boys do *not* cry. Ever.

Society has a clear set of rules and expectations for men and women about who they should be, and how they should and shouldn't behave. For men, there is one unrelenting message: don't be weak.

And it isn't only men who put pressure on each other. There's also a painful pattern that comes from women's expectations of men. Women ask men to be vulnerable and open up. Women plead with men to tell them when they're afraid, but the truth is that most women recoil with disappointment and disgust when it happens. I've experienced it, and so have many of my male clients. Men aren't stupid: we can see it in a woman's eyes.

So we hide. On goes the macho façade and our response to the shame we feel is either to react with anger or to shut down.

Two central societal themes make Manhood Shame especially hard and confusing today: the collapse of the materialist lifestyle model and the changing balance of the sexes.

When I started work 35 years ago, the 'job for life' had gone, but we knew if we worked reasonably hard and went to university, we could climb the corporate ladder and have a safe and secure career. Why would we ever consider another life? We didn't: we just blindly climbed on board!

Not any more. In the past decade alone, thousands of middle management positions have been cut due to technological advancement, along with the need to appease shareholders by reducing overheads and maximising profit. Younger generations are leaving university with huge debt, graduate unemployment levels are shockingly high, and most young people have been priced out of the housing market.

Whether we like it or not, the onus is still largely on the man to be the breadwinner, but looking forward it's increasingly unclear as to how that is going to be done: job security has gone.

On the face of it, this affects men and women equally. But there's one irrefutable difference between men and women: only women can give birth. Rightly or wrongly, it is still unusual for men to stay at home and look after the kids; paternity leave is relatively new and isn't equal to maternity leave.

I believe that having both parts of the couple working is a major reason for childhood stress, anxiety and depression. Households may have more money, but both parents come home shattered with significantly less time or emotional availability for their kids. Childhood security as provided by the family is not what it once was. For the feminist readers, I'm not saying that women should be chained to the kitchen sink, simply that this is an unforeseen consequence of more women working and the increasing financial burden of our have-it-all culture.

Let me declare up front: I am a feminist. I fundamentally believe in the equality of men and women. I believe in the equality of all human beings: black, white, gay, lesbian, bisexual, rich, poor and any other demographic you care to throw into the pot. There's no doubt that the balance is shifting hugely towards women and God knows it's long overdue.

However, there's a risk of downgrading the strength of what true femininity is, while only the arch-feminists, who insist on creating more separation, have a voice. Because of this, many men are too scared to take part in a conversation on equality. It is not disinterest. We understand the need for change while acknowledging that there's still a long way to go. The problem is that the strident feminist sends the average man into Manhood Shame and men will either react by getting defensive or by shutting down and avoiding, instead of participating in, the conversation. And it *is* men who need to change…their attitudes and their behaviours.

To get the genuine balance that the future requires, it is essential that men and women work *together*; we need the best of both to face the uncertain future of humanity, not pit against each other in the age-old battle-of-the-sexes. Men need to be allowed to be comfortable in their manhood: to be strong and dependable and yet empathetic and supportive.

It's up to us, the people on the street, to bring about social change. More than ever, partly thanks to the internet, we have a voice. But this means ordinary men and women - not just those with stronger views, bigger platforms and louder voices - taking to the streets, *together*.

More diversity, inclusion and mental health awareness need to be brought into schools and the workplace. The education system, which still prioritises academic intelligence over emotional and creative intelligence - skills required in the workforce of the future - needs an overhaul. Computers and A.I. will take over more and more of the basic tasks, so more emotional and creative thinkers are needed. And if we truly want a mentally healthy population, it starts with understanding and embracing our human emotions. Because boys *do* cry. Vulnerability is a strength, *not* a weakness. Being gentle and empathetic does *not* make you less of a man. And continuing a culture of stoicism, separation and egotism will ultimately lead to our demise, not progression.

Change a person; you change a culture. Change a culture; you change the world.

Reader Notes:

There are three key steps in any self-development programme that will allow you to stand tall:

❖ Self-Awareness – Slow down, pause and reflect. What makes you happy? What motivates you to get out of bed? What makes your heart sing? What's stopping you from being happy? Are you getting enough human connection? Are there enough close relationships in your life? Do you have friends who would 'put their life on the line for you'? How much time each week do you allocate for relaxation? What are your core values and are you honouring them? Bottom line: are you living a life you love? If not, what are *you* going to do about it?

❖ Self Esteem - Self-esteem is often confused with self-confidence, especially by men! Self-esteem is simply being comfortable in your skin and being happy with who you are, without the need to wear a mask and hide your true self. In my experience, few people have strong self-esteem, even those who appear happy and successful on the outside. You can excel yet still think you're useless; I did that for nearly 40 years! We worry far too much what other people think of us. The truth is, there are very few people who truly matter in your life, and within reason, they will love you anyway. And give me one solid reason why you *shouldn't* feel good about yourself. Yes, we've all failed, we've all done things we shouldn't have, we've all hurt people. Guess what: we're human! We all make mistakes. And we all get to learn the lesson, make our apologies if necessary and grow.

❖ Authenticity - Being authentic means expressing your *whole* self, including the parts you feel will be judged or rejected. It means not hiding but showing your vulnerability. Of course, we're brought up *not* to be vulnerable. We're told that it's a weakness, and men *cannot* be weak. But happily successful people always show their weaknesses: Richard Branson readily admits his dyslexia; Winston Churchill was perfectly open about his struggle with depression; Oprah Winfrey and Ruby Wax are honest about their struggles with mental health. Are these people weak? No! Being vulnerable is stepping into your own authentic power and it not only connects us to our inner humanity but to the humanity of others.

If you want to be a *real* man, understand who you are, accept who you are and stop hiding behind an inauthentic facade. Real men *are* emotional. They *do* cry. They do express all of their emotions and in healthy, constructive ways. When more of us men drop our macho masks and treat others with genuine respect, openness and empathy in all of our relationships, especially with women, the world will change!

About the Author:

Mark Newey is on a mission to eliminate stress, anxiety and depression. A self-avowed revolutionary in treating these mental health conditions, Mark has developed a unique programme – The Mark Newey Method.

After guiding himself through recovery from a breakdown and training in the neurosciences, Mark set up his own psychotherapy practice and over the last 18 years has helped thousands of people beat stress, anxiety and depression. He is now making this life-changing teaching available to all via seminars and a revolutionary online mental health programme.

Mark's upcoming book *'Kinship Rising: Healing Mental Health And Reconnecting Humanity'* and his online and offline community are helping him to spread the message and heal the world.

Connect with Mark:

Website: www.markneweymethod.com

Facebook: www.facebook.com/MarkNeweyMethod
Twitter: https://twitter.com/markneweymethod

Recommended Resources:

Websites:

www.ted.com/talks/brene_brown_on_vulnerability
www.ted.com/talks/brene_brown_listening_to_shame
www.ted.com/talks/simon_sinek_how_great_leaders_insp
ire_action?language=en

Books:

Daring Greatly by Brene Brown
A New Earth by Eckhart Tolle
The Biology of Belief by Bruce Lipton
Be More Pirate by Sam Conniff Allende
Age Of Anger by Pankaj Mishra
The Power Of Meaning by Emily Esfahini Smith

Feelings About Feelings
By Curtis Harren

'The greatest gift you can give somebody is your own personal development. I used to say, 'If you will take care of me, I will take care of you. Now I say, I will take care of me for you, if you will take care of you for me.' - Jim Rohn

Here I am, raw and exposed. When I heard about this project, I knew I had to share my story. Not because it's spectacular or brutal in any way, rather because it's probably very common. I grew up in a middle-class white household. My father worked, my mothers stayed at home, and I was one of two kids. I grew up knowing both of my grandparents. All three couples celebrated their 50th wedding anniversary. Even as a write this in the spring of 2018 I saw 25 years of marriage (well, nearly). I had a relatively 'normal' upbringing.

In the end, it doesn't matter. My story, your story; we all have one, and they *all* matter. Perhaps you've never thought of your life, or your experiences, as a story. Perhaps, by me sharing my mine you will come to see yours as well. The one thing I've come to realise recently is that no matter what our experience or background, they leave an indelible mark on our psyche and emotions. There is no competition between best or worst experiences in life. Everything is relative to ourselves and our own experience. Everything shapes our feelings, our decisions, our behaviour, and the patterns we choose every day regardless. If you get one thing from reading this chapter, I hope that it is that you can choose your future, and not be defined by your past.

My story

Like most men, I was raised to work hard, get a good job, help others and get shit done. I was never raised to be aware of my emotions or how to deal with them, except to push them to one side and get on with it. With one exception: anger, which was expressed freely. I was encouraged to punch a pillow, or go to my room and rage. It was even okay to yell at others because I was angry. But if I was sad I was told, 'It will be okay, it will get better, don't worry about it, it's just an emotion, it will pass'. Even when I was happy, it was never acknowledged or celebrated. I learnt that feelings didn't matter.

My upbringing wasn't abusive. For a while, my father had an unhealthy relationship with alcohol, but he wasn't an alcoholic. My mom was a stay-at-home mom and was always there. To coin a phrase, I had a true 'white picket fence' upbringing in middle-class Canada. We were not rich, but neither were we poor. We could not have anything we wanted, but if we worked hard enough, we could see the results of that effort. I grew up knowing both of my grandparents on both sides. My sister and I got along as good as any brother and sister. I grew up with a cat, and I grew up with a dog. See what I mean? Pretty nondescript. However, I came to realise that I had a very unhealthy relationship with my emotions. And while my childhood was 'normal', it still impacted my experience of life.

Emotional Turmoil

A few years ago, my then-wife asked for a divorce for the third time in our 20-year marriage. Emotionally I was torn apart. It was completely out of the blue. We'd only recently discovered that our early teenage daughter was self-harming and had written a suicide note. We had successfully taken her through the first steps of mental health support and were working on an active support plan. Things had begun to stabilise, Finally, it felt that our family was beginning to gel and unite again. Then BLAMMO! The divorce request knocked me for six and sent me into a tailspin.

I felt abandoned, betrayed, unsupported, confused, completely pissed off and done with life. It was during this time that I looked in an actual mirror, truly and honestly. I saw that I had a lot of personal work to do. I saw, since this was the third time, that maybe the common denominator was me. I was alone in the mirror; no one was behind me. You see, I'd fallen into the relationship trap that so many men do; I replaced all of my own friends with my wife's and their spouses. I had no real friends and felt completely isolated and alone. The emotions started to overwhelm me. I was heartbroken. Lost. Isolated. Betrayed. Disrespected. And, most of all, angry.

And I was frozen in fear. Due to our daughter's mental health situation and the fact that my consulting business was home-based, I became her personal chauffeur, guardian, support system, personal chef and everything in between. She was fully dependent on me. Yet in many ways, I had become co-dependent on her, neglecting my own wellbeing to be available at her beck and call. I pretty much shut down my business by prioritising my daughter. It seemed the right thing to do.

Then I was confronted with divorce: no friends, no income, no home of my own, no intimate relationship with my ex, and a tenuous relationship with my daughter. I haven't even mentioned my son, who was by now nothing but an afterthought, because 'he was good and we needed to focus on her'. I realise now how much guilt I carried back then for 'abandoning' him.

I was completely consumed, overwhelmed and crushed by

the most excruciating fear. At one point, while I was never suicidal, I became so overwhelmed by the flood of emotions that I couldn't breathe, sit, stand, eat or drink. I felt that I was going to vibrate until I exploded. Luckily, I had access to a support line through my ex's employee benefits plan. I remember little about the call I made, but I do remember knowing that the person on the other end would be following a script.

'I'm going to ask you not to follow your normal process. I don't want or need that; it doesn't work. Rather, I need you to go deep or ask questions that may not be comfortable for you, or me! Can you do that for me?' I asked. She agreed.

I will never forget when she finally asked the right question that broke through all the resistance to my innermost self. I had just shared the story of how, as a six-year-old, I was telling jokes to my family at a Christmas gathering. I messed it up. I forgot the joke, the punch line, the delivery. Everything. Everyone laughed. Not at the joke, *at me*! I felt unsupported, belittled, unloved and abandoned by my own family. The question she asked me was powerful, albeit simple: 'If you could go back in time and talk to yourself as that six-year-old boy, what would you say to him?'

Even now, many years later, I get the same reaction in my

body when I think about that experience. Even as I write this passage, my body reacts. The inside of my nose burns, my eyes well up in pre-tears, my vision dims, my heart expands, and it's a little hard to breathe. If I'm alone, I allow the tears. If I'm in public, I hold them back as best I can. At the time though, the intensity of my emotions was so strong that I almost lost all motor function. My body released all the bottled energy and emotion that I'd held onto my entire life. My legs gave out, and I collapsed to the floor. The phone bounced on the tile, and as I lay there, I could hear her voice asking: 'Are you alright? Hello? What happened?'. It took several moments before I could move my arms to grab the phone.

'That was it!' I said, 'That was the question I needed you to ask me! Thank you!'

You may be wondering what my answer to her question was. What *would* I say to my six-year-old self? 'I love you!' is the answer that came. 'You matter, you are important, and I'm here for you.'

Courage

'Courage, Dear Heart' - C.S. Lewis

What I learned from this experience was that my brain's reaction to my emotional pain was to go into fight or flight; it sensed danger and was trying to protect me. Because of the way I was raised, and the social setting I grew up in, I wasn't taught how to handle my emotions. In fact, is anyone? Isn't this why so many people self-medicate and self-harm through alcohol and other substance abuse etc? We very quickly learn that it isn't safe to show our emotions, so fight or flight becomes our default.

More significantly, I also learned that while I couldn't control the circumstances that caused my pain, I *could* control my experience and how I reacted to the feelings. In other words, I learned the difference between experiencing something that was happening versus something felt. I've since read and learned how this happens: our thoughts and feelings control or influence our behaviour and actions.

This meant I could have full control of my emotions in my head and not be afraid of them. I still felt them, even in their full intensity. I could see them for what they were: emotions. I could even identify where in my body I was experiencing them and how.

I realised, as a man, I wasn't living in my masculine energy. I was crushed by fear and overwhelmed by my emotions meaning I wasn't being authentic to myself. I decided during this experience that I would no longer live in fear. I would no longer shy away from my emotions. I would learn to live my own best life, for me! I took control and ownership of myself. I felt great, empowered, masculine and for the first time understood what it meant to be a 'real' man.

Nevertheless, I knew I would still feel fears and one fear, in particular, would plague me: being judged for being different. The fear of being persecuted, ridiculed and judged by other men, and possibly women, for being 'less of a man', 'more like a woman', 'a wuss', and so many more. As I started opening up and talking more, mostly with women, I realised the extent to which men were suppressed and even oppressed by their own emotions. I had myself tested as an abuser during therapy (more in this later), the verdict of which was that I wasn't an abuser, but I abused my emotions significantly. I realised that most men likely do this too, and it's destroying both the quality of their relationships - with themselves and others - and their lives. As a leadership coach, I wasn't living in integrity, and I needed to get the courage to face these fears and be a leader, for men *and* women, and mostly myself. I *decided* not to be fearless, but rather have the courage to feel my fears and emotions, no matter how overwhelming.

Vulnerability

'Vulnerability is not winning or losing; it's having the courage to show up and be seen when we have no control over the outcome. Vulnerability is not weakness; it is our greatest measure of courage.' Brene Brown, Rising Strong

Once I made the decision to face *all* of my emotions I knew this would alter how I experienced everything. What I didn't know was the extent to which I would feel. *Holy shit, did I feel!*

The thing is, once you experience an intense feeling or emotion there is an incredible desire to let it out. My alternative was to hold it in and bottle it. But as I'd discovered if I didn't release what I felt it would come back stronger, and probably inappropriately, often as rage, anger or resentment. I had to learn that other options and choices were available to me. I learnt to share my feelings with somebody, commonly known as vulnerability i.e. the willingness to open up and 'expose' my inner self to someone else. It's a hot mess to go through the first few times you experience this; some people are not receptive! I quickly learned who my real friends were and those who were not. It was easy to tell; the real friends listened and didn't run off.

Several years have passed since that phone call literally knocked the legs out from under me. Those years have seen hundreds of lifetimes and thousands of moments lived through. Personal development has that impact; a lot happens in a very short space of time. Contrary to popular belief, growth and change is not a smooth progression over time, neither linear nor sigmoidal; it's more like a slingshot. Change and growth engulf us and pulls, and pulls, and pulls. We are left in its clutches holding on to everything we can, our beliefs, our past, our ego, our identity, our hopes and dreams, our expectations, everything! Until we choose to either hold on tighter and have all that tension snapback on us leaving us scarred and poised to have the cycle happen again, or we let go and trust that we can fly on our own.

Growth happens very quickly, almost instantaneously. We launch ourselves to a new level very rapidly. This is what happened to me. I found that the more vulnerable I was, the more change I went through. The more change I went through, the more I learned about myself. The more I learned about myself, the more I grew. And the more I grew, the more I realised how little I knew about myself. It's a special kind of vulnerability to admit to oneself that you don't know who you are and own that without collapsing under the weight.

Going back to why I wrote this chapter, I realised that I wanted to inspire change in others. It's why I became a coach as a profession. I learned that opening up and sharing my hurt and my feelings with full vulnerability also opened up my wounds in a way that helped cleanse the wound so it would heal better and with less scarring (it was a very brilliant dear friend that observed this, thank you Wendy). This cleansing initially made me more sensitive, but I healed more wholly. So, I shared with whoever would listen. The damndest thing occurred. My business was taken more seriously. *I* was taken more seriously.

I used to say things like, 'I don't want the presentation to be all about me,' 'I don't have any good stories,' or, 'I can't reveal too much about myself.' The truth is I didn't want to be vulnerable. But it's worth the risk. People are drawn to the transformative power of vulnerability because it's rare to see someone share something so raw, especially a personal struggle.

For example; I recently madly, deeply and passionately fell in love with someone who didn't share my feelings, at least not in the same way. When our break up occurred, it was sudden and complete with no contact, leaving many festering wounds. Wounds that would reveal themselves in a store, with a breeze, at a picture, just a moment that triggered a memory, a thought, an unfulfilled desire or hope. The hurt I felt, and the pain I experienced was unfathomable and incredible. I chose to share this pain with select people along the way. By speaking my feelings, I healed a little more. Each telling revealed a little more of the hurt, a little more of the festering in my wounds. Even as I write this, many of these wounds are still open and bleeding, but I'm okay. I'm grateful to her for exposing these wounds, even for causing them. Because my feelings were so raw and strong, I knew they meant that every ounce of hurt I felt also reflected an equal measure of my ability to love. I realised that if I could hurt that much, I could, and did, love that much. Although the pain was excruciating at times, I didn't fear it; I felt it, every fucking ounce of it. I embraced the feeling. All my life I'd avoided feelings because they were uncomfortable, now I was truly enduring the most powerful agony ever. I couldn't breathe, or sleep. I couldn't focus, let alone function. Even now, I have to face this feeling arising in me at times, especially during a triggering event. She will always have a special place in my soul and heart for helping me find this in me.

Being willing to share my hurt and show my wounds to others helped me heal. Not because they fixed me, but because my sharing showed me I could handle it and that I was strong enough. It may even have attracted the very shining light I sought in another. Only time will tell on that front, but what I feel for her is so much more than what I felt for the other, but different because I can be honest with her and her with me. Was it worth it for me to be vulnerable? I don't even have all the evidence gathered, and I can categorically and emphatically scream YES! Oh my God YES!

Not only did I have to face myself on the inside, I had to face myself by sharing more of me to those on the outside. The deeper I allowed myself to go the more I started to love myself. These quotes say it all for me:

'He who would search for pearls must dive below.' - John
Dryden

*'Vulnerability is the only authentic state. Being vulnerable
means being open, for wounding, but also for pleasure. Being
open to the wounds of life, means also being open to the bounty
and the beauty. Don't mask or deny your vulnerability; it is
your greatest asset. Be vulnerable: quake and shake in your
boots with it. The new goodness that is coming to you, in the
form of people, situations and things can only come to you when
you are vulnerable, i.e. 'open!''* - Stephen Russell

Feel the Feelings

*'Being alone with your feelings is the worst because you have
nowhere to run. They're here, dancing in your mind and all
you can do is handle.'* - unknown

If I was to summarise what I learned most about myself and
the biggest transition of self-discovery, it's this: feel it.
Embrace every damn bit of it. Feel *all* the feelings. The joy,
the hurt, the anger, the sadness, the happiness, the
connection, the apathy, the frustration, the gratitude.
Absorb it all, for it is yours to behold. These feelings are
yours and yours alone. No one else's. They are your
greatest treasure for yourself and therefore your greatest
gift to yourself. They are the gateway to learn about who

you are and what you're capable of if you are '...*Brave Enough to be Vulnerable' (Unknown)*.

Especially with yourself. We too often think about being vulnerable with others. But to stand naked in front of yourself and fully expose your inner self to *you*, to admit your failings and fears, to admit your wrongdoings and your weaknesses takes real courage and vulnerability. These are frightening things, especially to our inner narcissist; we all have one. Only the true narcissist will never come to love the person behind that mask. The true narcissist will be so fearful of the feelings and stuff that comes up they will struggle to have the strength to face themselves and endure the wounds that are exposed. If you are reading this and have been hurt in a relationship with a narcissist, you will know the truth of this. If you are struggling to 'go there' for yourself or you're tired of crying and going to hurtful places inside of you, keep going. We are all rooting for you. I'm rooting for you. We all want you to find yourself. That is where inner peace lies, with total acceptance of all that you are and feel. The stillness, and joy, and pure love I feel. Wow. Just wow!

The Next Chapter

'Be Who you needed when you were younger' - unknown

Personal growth comes from personal acceptance. It was

truly powerful for me to tell my younger self that I loved him. But since that moment, well, I've done myself so much more. We all know actions speak louder than words. I've been able to show myself just how much I love who I am, and I get to fall in love with him, and who he is, every day. Even when I don't feel good about myself, and suffer doubts and even loathing, I get to truly learn who I am because I now accept and embrace the feelings I have about the feelings I have. And there is nothing more liberating than that!

I hope you've gleaned some insight from this chapter. Know that whatever has happened or is happening in your life, you're not alone. Know that facing your deepest fears and wounds takes true courage, vulnerability and strength. Know that expressing your emotions and exposing *all* that you are makes you more human, not less of a man.

Meet the Author:

Curtis Harren, CEOcopilot, is a creative and forthright experienced leadership development professional. His approaches to business are disruptive in the ways they are supposed to be. He is calm under fire, just him about ask about his Jeep, and he's a proven business turnaround specialist, especially by activating the people and the culture through vulnerability, honesty and transparency. He strongly believes that business is very personal and that should be embraced; it creates trust through authenticity and genuine concern for those around you. To him, work:life balance is achieved when the two are in sync and work together harmoniously and this requires the 'hardwork' of self discovery.

Connect with Curtis:

Website: www.ceocopilot.com

www.facebook.com/curtis.harren

www.linkedin.com/in/curtisharren

Being Vulnerable Is Your Superpower
By Scott Brandon Hoffman

'In the egoic state, your sense of self, your identity, is derived from your thinking mind – in other words, what your mind tells you about yourself: the storyline of you, your memories, the expectations, all the thoughts that go through your head continuously and the emotions that reflect those thoughts. All those things make up your sense of self.' ~ Eckhart Tolle

The piercing sound of screaming, yelling, and rage coming out of my father's mouth in the kitchen was so loud and intense that it felt like the roof was literally about to be blown off our house.

I was shaking, and so was my soul. I'm just a little boy. I'm scared. I don't feel safe. I don't feel happy. This is *not* the way it's supposed to be.

I have all these emotions inside me, swimming in my head and my body, but I don't know what to do with them. I feel alone and have no one to talk to about it. Part of me wants to run away. Part of me wants to hide. Part of me wants a hug and to know everything is going to be ok. It was like walking on glass when he was home, not knowing what mood he would be in or when he was going to explode next. So I felt scared, anxious, and on edge most of the time.

It was almost dinner time, and he and my mom were in the kitchen having a casual conversation about business, and everything seemed 'normal'.

The conversation got louder and louder and louder.

Mom had a big heart and tried to make peace in the house, but if she asked the wrong question or said the wrong thing at the wrong time (which was usually something that was true that my father didn't want to hear at that moment), it triggered him. He would go into an out of control fit of wild rage, and it usually ended up with more screaming to the point of bulging eyes, a beet red face, veins pulsating out of his head, and the fear that he would fall over dead from the sheer intensity.

But more likely, it would end with him racing through the house screaming and slamming doors, and ultimately storming out of the house to cool off.

This time was different.

Bang!

Smash!

The sound of dishes breaking into pieces.

Mom crying.

In his fit of rage, he threw a plate down on the table, and one of the pieces flew across and cut my innocent mother's wrist open. There was blood gushing everywhere, and she would have to be rushed to the hospital.

I ran into the kitchen to see what happened. I stood by my mom, and I looked at him with such anger (and fear), and I thought to myself, *sometimes I hate you, WTF is the matter with you? I love you, but why are you always so fucking angry?*

In The Beginning

We come into this world sweet, innocent, little Beings, full of love and joy, curious, happy, playful, authentic, gifted, and excited to go on this amazing ride called life.

We're sent from Creation Itself, and like all children, we are *pure love* in human form. Our Mission on this Earth is to be *fully ourselves* and to *shine our lights.*

In a healthy and loving environment, this is what happens to the lucky few, the problem is, it's *extremely* rare in our society. Unfortunately, there are a lot of wounded kids who turn into wounded adults and have no clue how to deal with their feelings, out of control emotions, and unchecked beliefs that they took on from childhood.

They don't understand what they're feeling, what drives their subconscious behaviour, and what makes them do what they do. They're unconscious and disconnected from a deeper understanding and the deeper part of themselves.

And one day while you're enjoying your life - having fun, dreaming of the future, and playing in the present - something happens. Somebody says something to you, or does something to you. You experience something bad, or you see something that hurts you. Things like sexual abuse, physical abuse, being a victim of racism, being bullied or beat up at school, being in a car accident, being yelled at, being made fun of, being ignored, rejected, ridiculed, or laughed at, to give some examples.

We have all kinds of experiences in the early years and throughout our lives that can shake us to the core. They can be little things that feel big to us or traumatic things that are life-threatening. *All* these things affect us and shape our beliefs and behaviours.

You have a thought, an emotion, a feeling, and you want to express it; it's part of being human, and you deserve to feel safe to do so. And you want to tell your dad, a teacher, a group of 'so-called' friends, a girl, society, or even your mother, and somebody at some time in your early life ultimately says to you implicitly or explicitly: 'Just Man Up and Get Over It.'

That's when it starts.

The damage that would inevitably ignite the downward spiral that makes so many of us, beautiful children, little kids, teens, young adults, and men put on our first mask. We cover up, stay silent, go into depression, and flirt with anger and rage. We bury our feelings and true individual Soul expression for good (or, at least, until we decide to take back our power and *live* our truth).

It's game on.

We move our pain into the spiritual basement of our Soul because we learned that it's not okay to be ourselves, to speak up, to show our feelings, emotions, and fears.

The result?

We start feeling alone, not good enough, full of shame and believe there's something wrong with us. We don't fit in, and learn 'I can't be myself' without being judged, teased, yelled at, ignored, beat up, or laughed at.

Here's the truth: *everyone* has insecurities, *everyone* feels pain in their lives about something, and most people live two lives, the one they show you in public, and the one they feel and live in private.

All these feelings and emotions add up, and it's easy for us to decide to shut down or to create limiting beliefs born from fear and unworthiness; it's a protection mechanism, and it comes with a price.

We all want to be accepted, feel like we belong somewhere, find our identity, our joy, our gifts, and some meaning to all this craziness in life. And the first thing we want in life is to be loved by our fathers (and mothers), and we'll do anything to make it happen, even it means losing ourselves for a while.

Deep down we all want to be seen, heard, loved, feel safe, and feel like we belong. But because of all the pain we experience in one form or another, we turn to the mask and don't let anyone see the real us because we weren't taught to express our true selves. Instead, we play a role, we pretend, we hide, we put on a fake smile, we have shame, and we suffer inside because of it. Some of us even hate ourselves.

That's how damaging it can be.

Then we go searching and looking for role models in the 'real world' on how to be a *real* man. We look to our fathers, celebrities, men in business, athletes, or rock stars, some version that society and the media put on a pedestal and calls successful. We buy into and start chasing whatever we think will make us finally feel 'good enough' or be 'loved enough.'

Our subconscious mind works to match what we currently think about ourselves and the world, and most of the time, until we're conscious and awake, it's not a match to the truth of who we *really* are.

We come to this world completely innocent, open, with tender hearts filled with joy, and then through no fault of our own, we pick up messages, programs, beliefs, words, harmful experiences, traumas, and false ideas that go *deep* into our subconscious mind, our brain, and our souls, from wounded people.

It takes over our reality.

And our egos and brains do everything they know how to keep us safe. Sadly for most of us that means *not* being who we truly are and being afraid to express what we really feel. *This* is why we suffer. We're disconnected from our souls.

We shut down, get depressed, or we rage with anger and rebel. We become overachievers so we can feel good about ourselves and have people praise us, or we hide in isolation so nobody sees us because we think we don't deserve to be seen. It often turns into unhealthy addictions like alcohol, drugs, sex, domination of women, living on social media, fighting, and in the worst cases, ending our own lives through suicide.

It's just wrong.

We do anything and everything to distract ourselves from our feelings and to get us to feel temporary (or permanent) relief, pleasure or distraction to numb out the pain. This is what most of the world does on a daily basis, and it's sad, but there is a way out of the loop. We need to understand where it all comes from, how it works within the brain, the emotions, psychology, and the subconscious mind, and what you can do about it to no longer feel alone or live in shame.

The key - for boys, men, adults, *all* of us - is to understand first and foremost that it's okay to feel what you feel, *even if* you're a man, because you're human. We *all* have feelings and emotions; they're not just for the girls and women. We have fucking hearts too. Then you can address the pain, take back your power and begin to turn your life around. You are *always bigger* than any of your stories, pain, and emotional struggles.

This is important to hold on to because we lose too many young men and older men to suicide or death through drug and alcohol addictions because they don't see a way out past their emotional pain. But I'll say it again: there is - *always* a way out. Remember this truth somewhere deep in your heart and soul.

Turning Off My Lights

We've had what can feel like several lifetimes of negative

programming embedded in us that has screwed a lot of us up and beat our joy, longings, dreams, desires, passions, and our voice and truth right out the back door, leaving us looking for it along with our lost innocence.

When I grew up, like most of us, I was a little bundle of joy. I came here imprinted with my unique gifts, creativity, personality, talents, and big heart. I was a huge light, full of energy and joy, always laughing and making other people laugh. I was a born entertainer, front and centre of every room putting on a show for whoever was there. I loved music (I've been playing the piano since I was five), and photography (I was getting paid professionally aged 10). I was a little comedian, and was very artistic, conscious, and spiritually awake but didn't understand what it was because no one in my house nurtured that part of me. They didn't really 'get' me, so I kept it to myself.

I had an artist's soul, an entertainer's personality, and I was sensitive to energy and the environment around me because I was awake, and it was a hard place to be for me. I could light up a room, a stage, and the world, and feel into your soul and know precisely what you were feeling and what was going on inside you. I was a little empath.

But like so many of us - through witnessing and feeling all the dense energy in my house, the experiences at school, unhappy kids lashing out, the teasing, the yelling, the raging, the bullies, the not feeling safe, the not belonging, the dysfunctional conversations and actions - I unconsciously chose to shut down and turn off my lights. I didn't have an outlet to express it or talk about it, so I gave it my own meaning and said, 'Fuck it, this is what we do.'

I decided somewhere in my little head that I was unworthy, that there was something wrong with me, that I must be unlovable, and not good enough. So I reached for a mask, a story, and some limiting beliefs that I would wear and act out for decades.

I hid my pain in school by being the comedian, making a joke out of everything to deflect my fear of not fitting in or being beat up by the big kids. I just wanted to be accepted, so I found a way to do it. One of the ways was laughter, and the other was playing in a rock band.

When I was on stage playing music, I felt like I was home. I felt safe up there, and all the cool kids, including the jocks and the beautiful girls, looked up to me because I had a gift. I still didn't feel good enough inside because I had these old tapes running in my head. I was still insecure, but the music was part of my soul, so it fed me. It was part of the real me, that part that can wake us up and heal us.

As a small child I subconsciously decided that the world wasn't safe. My home didn't feel safe; school didn't feel safe. I didn't feel loved, seen, heard, understood, appreciated, good enough, or nurtured…*all* the things that make a healthy, confident, high self-esteem child, teen, and adult. I took my programming deep into my mind and played it out in the world, *every single day* for years.

After the plate throwing accident, I could see in my dad's eyes how bad he felt and how sorry he was. He was really a teddy bear with a huge heart inside who loved my mother deeply, and who had unchecked emotions underneath his own buried pain. Nobody was ever physically hurt or intentionally emotionally hurt in my house. We were a typical, nice suburban family that loved each other in our own way and who happened to be a little dysfunctional - welcome to pretty much all the families in the world.

I know now that he would never hurt anyone, and he never has. He loved us all more than his own life, but sometimes because of his deep repressed emotions in the past, and not having an outlet for them, he resulted in a fit of rage. Even now there are times I wish I'd had the courage to run up to him when I was small, hug him and say, 'I love you Daddy', or to have him come to me and say, 'I love you Scotty, I'm here for you, I believe in you, you can be and have anything you want in this world, you are a gift, you are special.'

There are no excuses for unacceptable behaviour in life. I am all about boundaries and speaking the truth now, but as little kids, we don't really understand this. We want love and safety. This is what drives people to unintentionally and sometimes intentionally hurt other people in ways without knowing what the repercussions of it will be.

We live in a world of humans with all kinds of feelings and emotions, and most aren't conscious enough to know how to deal with them in a healthy way. So many of us have no understanding of what we're actually feeling inside, and can blow up at the slightest trigger, or stuff it down and go silent as it slowly eats us from the inside out.

This is why you see so many bullies and kids picking fights in school, doing drugs, trying to get attention, or feeling depressed. They're in pain because they're afraid and lack love and presence in their lives, mostly their family lives, so they act out or shut down; we see it everywhere.

In my home environment, we just weren't encouraged to talk about our feelings, heart's desires, problems, emotions, dreams, or spend time in long loving nurturing hugs, or hear 'I love you' consistently enough.

So I did what a lot of us do. I shut down. Went numb. Turned my lights off. Hid. Felt unworthy and not good enough. Played small. Didn't make too much noise, be too happy or unhappy. I hid my feelings from the world, instead wearing a mask of pretence. I hid the real me because I felt I was inferior and didn't deserve to be happy or feel good.

These are *all* lies that I told myself and that we as a collective tell ourselves.

And to be clear, they *are* lies.

We take the pain into our everyday experience as little kids, teenagers, young adults, adults, and even into old age, and if we don't wake up, it runs us and hold us back until we take our last breath and leave this planet. We think it's normal to feel this way, but it is *not* normal to stuff down your feelings. It's a symptom of unhealthy programming, limiting beliefs, and self-hatred.

This is why you see so much chaos in the world; fighting, wars, sexual exploitation, and people acting out in all kinds of crazy ways. It's people living from their pain and not their hearts that causes the problems.

If we could have a collective voice of truth from the world's children, it might sound like this:

'What the fuck is wrong with our society that people are *so* unconscious, *so* unhappy, *so* lacking in joy and self-love, *so* miserable with no meaning or purpose, and being *so* unwilling in their lives to do the work to reconnect to their hearts and true selves? They're not dealing with their shit. They act out and pour it onto everyone they love, work with, and even their own little innocent children, and scar them for life.'

This is why I do the work that I do.

We have an epidemic in the world of people walking around hurting, feeling numb, distracted, angry, depressed, in pain and not understanding where it's coming from or what they can do about it to feel better and to live an amazing life with self-love at the centre.

Burying Our Truth

So why do we wear these masks and bury our truth?

We're afraid to expose ourselves.

We're afraid to be seen.

We're afraid to let people know we have flaws and struggles because we're supposed to be Instagram perfect with happy smiley faces 24/7.

We're supposed to be strong, courageous men who take on the world.

We're programmed and in a hypnotic trance from our agenda and consumer-driven society that couldn't give a shit about what truly makes us happy. It only wants what it wants: numbed out, obedient consumers and sheeple who don't think too much, feel too much, say too much, or stir up any trouble. They want us to hate ourselves and think we're broken, so they can sell us shit we don't need to fix us when we're not broken in the first place. This reality is part of the human condition.

I have learned over the years to have compassion for *all* people: the moms, the dads, the teachers, the other kids, the bullies, the adults. They're all acting out from their wounds, their pain, and what they took on from an unawakened world or a dysfunctional family.

Hurt people, hurt people.

Most people don't know what they don't know. Pain and limiting beliefs get carried over and passed down from generation to generation until someone decides to wake up and *do* something about it.

I always felt unworthy. I had no confidence and self-esteem. I didn't like myself let alone love myself; I even hated myself for a time. I had a lot of built up anger in me, especially when I was younger. I was wearing a macho, BS mask, pretending to be okay, acting tough and playing a role, wearing a fake smile and having a laugh, when in fact there was a scared, pissed off little boy inside me running my life and holding me back from living in my highest joy.

Our early programming runs us and our lives until we become self-aware enough, present enough, in pain enough, and *brave* enough to shine a light and say, *I'm done with this old way of being. I'm tired of fighting with myself, feeling like shit, and living in pain and quiet desperation. I want to change! I want to feel good!*

I spent the majority of my life not even understanding why I felt and acted the way I did until I finally had enough. It's taken me 20+ years of inner work - diving into every personal development book, video, audio and learning *all* the tools - to turn a corner and feed into the truth of my being, and now I'm coaching and mentoring others to do the same.

I'm still a work in progress. I'm not perfect. I still battle the residue of my demons; we *all* do. There is no, 'I finally got it, I'm done.' New insights and evolving is part of the long-term plan, so embrace it. But being conscious, aware, and having tools changes the game *instantly.*

Giving Yourself Permission

Give yourself permission to feel, to not be afraid of your pain, to get comfortable with discomfort, to wake up and start to change your life at any moment. The decision is yours; it's always a choice.

Say this to yourself now:

IT'S OK TO FEEL.

I GET TO talk about how I feel and not feel shame or weak.

I GET TO change my life.

I GET TO be happy.

I GET TO come alive and feel joy.

I GET TO express myself.

I GET TO be supported.

I GET TO feel loved.

I GET TO know that I am enough.

I GET TO love myself.

I GET TO forgive *all* the people who hurt me. They didn't know better; they only did their best with what they had at the time. It's not about them anyway, they were just wounded, hurt little kids acting out on themselves.

I HAVE THE POWER IN ME, and I choose to let my old stories go and my old ways of being go, for my health and wellbeing.

For me, I can see it clearly now through the lens of compassion. All the things that were said or done to me in grammar school, high school, and college, all the things that hurt me, and the things I said to hurt them back, all came from our fears and wounds.

My childhood was far from perfect, and not the way I would have wanted it to be as a kid, but I understand that it is *all* perfect now because I see through a different perspective and lens. I've done the inner healing work and shown myself what's actually true.

You have to be willing to look at your darkness, your shadows, and your pain because it is in there that you will find the light. The pain in life is helping us grow into the beings that we were created to be on this planet. So it starts with recognising that it's okay to feel, that there's nothing wrong with you, and there is a better way to live.

There's a way that aligns with and ignites your soul, turns your lights on, and allows you to share your feelings, clear your pain, come alive and be who you were born to be. It starts with confronting and letting go of the untruths that you no longer choose to hold on to out of fear, safety or protection, and to uncover the *real* truth so that you can finally be yourself – *all* of you - and live the life that you were born to live without feeling bad anymore. You can become that example in the world for others to admire and

...model because you're authentic and real. This can save your own life and possibly the lives of countless others.

Lies, Lies, Lies

Recognise some of these?

➤ Don't ever cry; it's a sign of weakness.

➤ Never let people know you're afraid.

➤ Bury your emotions.

➤ Your feelings are in your head, get over it and man up!

➤ Feelings are for girls.

➤ If you're gay, you're a sinner.

➤ Don't be vulnerable or people will think you're a pussy.

➤ Don't let anybody disrespect you or you'll have to show 'em what's up.

➤ You have to be cool, rich, successful, and macho to be 'somebody' and to have women attracted to you and to love you.

➤ Don't be different; nobody likes different. Be normal like everyone else.

➤ You'll never make it in the world as an artist, a creative, or doing what you love.

- Don't be sensitive.

- Screw your heart, do whatever it takes to be successful, and make money at all costs. Otherwise you're a loser in the world's eyes, and in your family's eyes, and maybe even secretly in *your* own eyes.

I played this role well. I hid for years, decade. I played out the patterns that I adopted from my childhood. I remained in isolation, in pain, battling depression and angry rebellion on and off, and not playing full out in the world or living my dreams. The little boy in me didn't feel good enough, and he was pissed off, felt rejected, unseen, unloved, and he played out by sabotaging everything.

This is how the subconscious part of us acts out. If you don't align with that part of you - your inner child (your soul and your heart) - listen to it, and give it what it needs, deserves, and wants, then you will be fighting with parts of yourself for the rest of your life. Your heart, your soul, your inner child are your way back to happiness and true self-expression; your Spiritual GPS.

When I was feeling down my dad would say, 'Pick your boots up by the straps and get back out there. Don't let anyone see your fears or weakness. Buy some new clothes, and go be successful,' and he would tell me the wisdom from his grandmother who he loved so much. He was saying it all out of love. He didn't understand that I had emotions and feelings that needed to be expressed, and I was too scared to talk about it for fear of being judged or shut down again, so he gave his advice based on his way, and I took it in.

But know this (and I will keep reminding you of this over and over):

It's OK to feel and have feelings.

It's OK to have emotions.

It's OK to cry.

It's OK to talk about your shit.

There is *nothing* wrong with you.

We've all been programmed since birth to live as we're *expected* to be from the media, movies, fairy tales, celebrities, magazines, and consumerism that has knocked us all off of our centre in one way or another. It's driven by completely false and unrealistic expectations. It's even caused the boom in the self-help industry and the cosmetic surgery industry, among others, so we can 'fix' what's wrong with us and live up to these expectations and beliefs that society places on us.

It's all a fucking lie.

This is the cancer that has spread to so many human beings, feminine and masculine alike, in the name of consumerism to sell shit we don't need. We have suffered quietly and endlessly for generations through the demand of false programming and dysfunctional, unconscious behaviours for far too long because of the intense expectations, programming, and exploitations put upon us.

Men are supposed to be rich, handsome, have big muscles, be stoic and have it all together, drive fancy cars, bang their chests to show their power, be sports fanatics and outdoor adventurers, successful, famous, and have a supermodel by their side. Life is messy, none of us is perfect, there is *no* perfect, and there is *no* one way of being.

Most of us have been wearing our masks for a lifetime while suppressing and hiding our true selves, and that in of itself is exhausting. It's time to let go.

I don't care if you're five or 80 years old. You *always* get to be yourself. Period. It's time to take off your mask, take a risk, show us the real you. The *authentic* you. The *unmasked* you. Show us the part of you that doesn't feel good enough or worthy enough. I want to see *all* of your flaws. I want to see *all* of your imperfections. I want to see *all* of your hopes and fears. I want to see *all* of your struggles and pain. I want to see *all* of your heart.

Because when you let it out and put it on the table, it loses its power, and will ultimately set you free. When we can let go of what other people think of us, and not care about being judged or afraid of being seen as too vulnerable or weak, we're free. Living undefended and authentic is your fucking superpower. When you can live with courage, strength, vulnerability, authenticity, and be comfortable in your skin without the need to impress anybody let alone the world, you're free.

Hiding your heart and true self is painful, exhausting, and it's macho bullshit.

It gets to end now.

Nobody is at fault. Life is happening as it does for a multitude of reasons, and ultimately, it is for us to grow and expand as souls. Being vulnerable, present, speaking your truth, sharing love is *always* the right thing to do. The goal is that fear and old ways of being don't get to run your heart anymore; love does. And it's never too late to be open and real with your feelings and to love. In the end, my father was a great man on his own soul path. He had a big heart. He opened and evolved more and more as he grew older and learned how to express his feelings and his love openly. It was beautiful to witness, to see who he really was. Underneath that old guarded mask that he wore was a beautiful, big-hearted, sensitive man who loved his family more than life itself.

We did a lot of talking and a lot of healing throughout the years, and I saw that little five-year-old boy in him just as I still see it in myself. The power of a father and son's love will always be in our soul, no matter what, so give yourself that gift to talk and express before it's too late. My dad passed away in 2012, and he left his love, courage, strength, sense of humour, lessons, and his legacy behind in me.

I love you Dad, thank you for all the gifts you've given me; I wouldn't change a thing.

Becoming a Real Man

Real Men:

➢ Express their feelings and sensitivity.

➢ Know their vulnerability is a sign of courage and power, not weakness.

➢ Know that asking for help is a sign of strength.

➢ Have and share tremendous amounts of love, compassion, empathy, and joy.

➢ Are present.

➢ Follow their hearts, do what they love, and have a mission and passions that light them up and add real impact to the world.

- Stand strong in the name of love even when they're afraid.

- Stand up for their partner, their family, their purpose, and *always* aim to do the right thing.

- Aren't afraid to show their feelings to other men and have deep, authentic, real conversations and support each other.

- Give their hearts to the people around them and the world.

- Are powerful, conscious, and sensitive beings who aren't afraid to show *all* of themselves, feelings included, and be who they were born to be.

- Love and appreciate themselves.

- Aren't afraid to cry.

  (I cried like a baby in front of my girlfriend and men friends on and off for six months, after my mother died. There is no shame.)

  This is how I live my life now after *all* the inner work and healing I've done. It's not about perfection, but always moving in the right direction, being conscious of who you be and how you show up, and doing your best to choose the higher road in each moment.

  This is the new lens for being a *real* man. I want to share this with the world and give permission to as many boys and men as possible to adopt, so we can all be healthier versions of our most authentic selves and change our lives and the world for the better.

The new man, the *real* man, the heart-centred man, the conscious man is powerful, mission and purpose-driven, vulnerable, strong, sensitive, and a total badass of love, compassion, empathy, creativity, and leadership.

We're taking our power back.

We're waking up.

We're seeing behind the curtain and exposing the illusion of expectations, perfection, the programming, and the lies.

We're *remembering* the truth.

We're beginning to understand what happened to us in our childhoods, how it's shaped us, how it runs us, and how our thoughts and beliefs create our lives. We're taking back our power and understanding the truth beyond the experience or the stories in our minds. Knowing that we are all good enough, worthy enough, and perfect exactly as we are *without* our masks.

It's an ongoing process; there is no arriving. We're human beings after all. We'll experience pain by the very nature of being human. But who you become every day from talking and expressing more of your truth and living from your heart will change who you *be* and your life.

We are *all* children of God and are worthy of a great life.

This is not typical boys or men talk I know. You won't hear this in school locker rooms, in the boardroom, or at home, but it's true. It's necessary. And it's becoming the norm for what *real* men talk about and *need* to talk about.

There is a movement of men's and young men's groups happening around the world because of the realisation that talking, expressing, and being heard is necessary for our health and wellbeing.

What we really want is closeness, connection, love, compassion, true self-expression, acceptance, authenticity, to be seen, to be heard, to live our own truth, to belong, to create, to stand spiritually naked with empathy for all (including ourselves), and to not be afraid to let people see who we truly are.

This is our time. This is *your* time.

No more stuffing feelings. No more hiding. No more playing small. No more hidden rage and anger. No more disconnection from your heart, life, and the people you love. No more letting distractions and fears run you.

You get to feel and be all of you. You get to heal the past.

It's time to let go, be true to yourself and set yourself free.

Readers Notes:

<u>My Soul Prescription</u>

It really boils down to three things to change your life.

- ❖ Self-Awareness *and* the willingness to make a decision and a commitment that you're ready to change and that you *can* change, however long it takes.

- ❖ Daily Self Love.

- ❖ Doing the work.

So you've made a decision and a commitment that you're finally ready to take on feeling good and freeing yourself from the old programming, the patterns, and the stories that have kept you stuck and in emotional pain. Congratulations! Old habits don't die easily, so go easy on yourself.

Here's where you can start:

First be willing to be brutally honest with yourself. It's time to be present and get real, and it's okay if it feels uncomfortable, because it will. You're going to threaten the ego mind's identity and stories, and it's going to fight for its life.

Next, drop into your heart and listen to what it's telling you. Ask yourself these two questions:

What isn't working in my life?

What do I *really* want?

Do not filter it, and do not listen to the noise in your head because that's the wrong part to listen to. This isn't about blame and shame. This is about your heart and soul here. Let that little kid in you talk and have his voice heard, listen to the dreams, desires, fears, and pains etc. This is the part of you that has felt rejected, hurt, ignored and pissed off. This is the part of you that's been acting out and making you feel the way you do. Listen to *all* of it. Sit with it and listen.

Once you've done this, you're one step closer to setting yourself free.

When you know what's not working *and* you know what you want, then it becomes about doing the three steps above consistently.

Whenever you feel bad or down again, don't fight it. Just accept it, love it, listen to it, and then drop back into your heart and ask, 'What do I need to know? What is it telling me?'

Whenever you resist something that you want, tune in and see what the limiting belief is. Whatever the excuse or story that says you can't have it or be it, is your limiting belief. Make a new decision that empowers you to be the person that gets to have what you want and allows and trusts in the Universe and yourself.

This is the practice. The heart is your spiritual guidance system. It will teach you, lead you, heal you, and ultimately bring you home to self. Trust it like your life depends on it because it does.

About the Author:

Scott Brandon Hoffman Empowers and Entertains people to:

'TURN THEIR LIGHTS ON and COME ALIVE.'

He's performed on stage with A listers like Wayne Brady, coached and trained high level CEO's as well as top influencers and celebrities, and spoken at corporations such as Southwest Airlines.

Scott's a featured writer for the Good Men Project and the Hollywood Journal among others, and has been on radio shows and podcasts across the world.

He's a Conscious, Heart Centered, Transformational

Speaker, Singer, Songwriter, Spoken Word Artist, Comedian, Entrepreneur, and Kickass Coach and Mentor; a one of a kind Artist, Entertainer, and Visionary Leader on a BIG mission to Impact Millions Of Lives.

Through his bold, heartfelt, innovative, and rare blend of Original Music, Entertainment, Speaking, Storytelling, Coaching, Comedy, and Life Changing Wisdom, he empowers and inspires his audiences and clients worldwide to LOVE deeply, to Live their TRUTH, to Express Themselves, Own Their Voice, Step Into Their Creativity, and to PLAY and LAUGH again, ultimately to COME FULLY ALIVE, and to FINALLY set themselves FREE.

Connect with Scott:

www.ScottBrandonHoffman.com
www.facebook.com/ScottBrandonHoffmanLive
www.instagram.com/ScottBrandonHoffman
www.twitter.com/TheEntertainer

Recommended Resources:

Books:

The Mask of Masculinity by Lewis Howes
Breaking The Habit Of Being Yourself by Dr. Joe Dispenza
The Untethered Soul by Michael A. Singer

The Power Of Vulnerability by Brene Brown
The Power by Rhoda Byrne
The 5 Second Rule by Mel Robbins

Websites:

The Good Men Project: www.goodmenproject.com
Garrain Jones: www.facebook.com/Garrainjones
Evan Carmichael:
www.youtube.com/channel/UCKmkpoEqg1sOMGEiIysP
8Tw
Will Smith:
www.youtube.com/channel/UCKuHFYu3smtrl2AwwMO
XOlg
Kyle Cease: www.kylecease.com

The Bumpy Road to Success
By Reece Formosa

'Our greatest glory is not in never falling, but in rising every time we fall.' ~ Confucius

From a young age, I dreamed of success. I grew up in a typical blue-collar family from the middle-class suburb of Tea Tree Gulley, Adelaide, Australia. My father ran a crash repair business while Mum raised us boys. Our family business didn't make lots of money, but our parents always had a way to make us feel rich.

I clearly remember Dad finding an old bike at the dump, fixing it up as if it was brand new and giving it to me for my 6th birthday. Little did I know that we were struggling financially. Eggs on toast for dinner was common and if we were lucky a trip to the local fish and chip shop was on the cards. We did get to spend loads of time travelling in their camper van at the river.

In 1996 the family business went into voluntary liquidation, and I was left confused as to why I couldn't go and help Dad in his shop anymore. Dad went to work for the government and Mum took a recruitment job. I was none the wiser, but my brothers and I had to move school. We were in a private school, and my parents couldn't afford the fees anymore. This to me was fine. I hated that school anyway and made a lifetime of new friends at my new one.

For years I dreamt about one day owning my own business. I wanted nothing more than to be successful.

By the age of 15, I decided to be an electrician. I set out to do work experience with a local guy who eventually took me on as his apprentice. After a few months working with him, I discovered he wasn't the best person to work for; his work ethics and safety standards were questionable.

I left and joined a far more professional company. They had good systems in place, but the owner was frivolous with his money, owning all the toys in the world and a holiday house at the river. Eventually, his company went bust, and I was without a job. I was 18. I seemed to be drifting further from my dream.

With only one year of my apprenticeship remaining, I took a role at a company which, from the outside, looked very promising for a long career. Then the global financial crisis hit. The majority of large electrical companies in Adelaide folded along with all the small companies before them. I had the worst luck possible in the early stages of my career. Nothing was going right.

An opportunity to work as a home theatre installer came up, and given my electrical skills, I was the perfect fit for the role. I applied, got the job, and loved it. Working in mansions installing home theatres was a thrill and very inspiring. My dream ignited some more. After two years I realised I could do this myself and started my first real business - Unique Home Theatre - which is still operating today.

My home theatre business was booming. I was onto something good here. In my first year, I turned over $80,000, incredible for a 20-year-old who knew fuck all about business. I was living the dream! The following year I doubled my sales and by year three almost doubled them again. I was making more money than the teachers who said I'd be a dropout all my life.

Two years into this business I met someone who would eventually cause more issues for me than I expected. He was young (27), successful and had money, or so I thought. We started a small tech company to develop an electronic key finding device. He would be my senior advisor and mentor.

We raised some private investment and went off to build the device. We ended up being ripped off and spending over $150k of personal and private money to complete the product. We had a prototype and plan but no idea how to take it to market. Companies were asking for thousands of orders, but we didn't have the capital to make the purchase orders. I remember leaving a meeting in Melbourne after an agent of Apple ordered 10,000 units. I said yes, then called my partner to find out the company had no money to fulfil the order.

Another blow. Another disappointment.

I almost cried (but didn't).

The Day That Changed Everything

I was using my home theatre business to fund the development of the key finder, and as a result, wasn't seeing a good return for my efforts. My business partner decided to take out a lease on a warehouse that, in reality, we couldn't afford. None of the other people in our little business group knew about it until we rocked up and he had the keys in his hands. Instantly, we were all financially worse off; it was roughly $2k each per month to have this office.

Six months passed and I was making decent money at my home theatre business. But the beginning of 2014 brought with it a day that changed *everything.*

I was working on a job with my brother installing this amazing system in a house in one of the more upper-class suburbs of Adelaide. The house was amazing. We worked on the system for a few days, and on the final day, we had one cable run to finish. I marked out the wall for drilling and put my drill into the wall - right into a mains water pipe. Now, I can promise you this: the pipe was *not* meant to be there by any builder's standards. The living room started to flood. Within seconds the whole of the floor in this multi-million-dollar home was an inch deep in water.

I drove off to collect the tools needed to fix the mess. On my way back, I pulled up at the lights and looked into my rear mirror. A car was racing towards me with no sign of slowing down. BAM! It hit me. The emergency services arrived, my brother collected the equipment from me to fix the water, and I was taken to hospital.

When I awoke the following day, I couldn't walk. I was in agony. I had twisted my back and damaged my L3 disk. I was out of work according to the doctor. Hell was all I could see. I wasn't able to ride my bike, I couldn't drive. I couldn't do anything. Just rest in bed.

A major setback. But still, I didn't cry.

Hitting Rock Bottom

The business went downhill from there. Jobs couldn't be finished, money wasn't coming in, and I had no vision for the future. My relationship broke down because as humans we take our issues out on our loved ones. I slipped into depression. Months went by. I was tens of thousands of dollars behind on bills and my electricity at my house was about to be turned off. I remember thinking, *at least they can't turn my water off.*

Demand letters piled up, and I couldn't make phone calls to arrange payment plans; I could only receive calls. I was laying on the couch watching TV. It turned off. A guy was running across my lawn. I confronted him. 'Pay your bills,' he demanded. I felt like a loser. Here's me, the successful entrepreneur with over $100k of debt, bills that couldn't be paid, no clear path to income and a warehouse we had rented for no reason. This wasn't the success that my younger self had dreamed of all those years before.

The only choice I had was to come up with something that would make me money. And fast. So I hustled. I started selling everything: clothes, jewellery, *anything*. I remember putting $50 cash into my wallet and feeling rich again.

For a year I struggled. I was fighting with my parents because they didn't know the full story and the debt I was in. My dad and I had issues over me not working, but I tried to explain that I needed to rest. He is an old-school Maltese man whose work ethic is like no other, so 'lazing' on the couch was not a good look.

Eventually, I couldn't take the pain anymore. I went to my doctor, and he suggested - off the record - that I try smoking cannabis. I tried it for the first time since leaving High School. I slept the best I had in two years.

Cannabis also made me hungry, so I started using the little cash I was earning to order pizza. Soon I was tired of pizza and wanted another home delivery solution. I was at a friends house with a group, incredibly stoned and talking about life. I suggested we start a company that delivers anything you want via an app.

We landed on Delivery Boyz, and I set off to work on the business given I had fuck all else to do at the time. I had laser focus and one goal: sell the business to On The Run (OTR), the local billion dollar company everyone looked up to. I couldn't literally see the process of me selling it to them in my mind. It was like I had a vision into the future. Fast forward six months, the business had launched, and customers were using us. We even won a local award for best start-up.

I met Shane later that year; we hit it off. He was the local entrepreneurial success story. He'd won a few awards and was - according to him - very rich. I suggested I eventually sell the delivery business to OTR or get them to invest, so he set up a meeting. OTR invested after some due diligence, and we set off to build a good start-up.

While all of this was going on, I still had a mountain of issues piling up related to the warehouse we had and the tech business we'd started. So I made a decision. I was going to run the delivery business and let my business partner run the key finder business. He was very keen to do this, so we drafted the paperwork for me to resign as director and we focused on our separate ventures. I built Delivery Boyz to over $1,000,000 per year, but we were not making any money. It was a low margin business and, eventually, when Uber came along, we got whipped out the market (I later sold my share of the business to OTR at the end of 2017).

A New Day, A New Disaster

'Reece, can you drop me off at the BMW garage to get my car serviced?' said my business partner.

'Sure mate,' I said. And off we went.

The salesman showed us their latest range. 'Do you like this new M3 we have for sale?' he asked. My business partner replied, 'Yes I do'. I knew he wanted it, so reminded him how much debt we had to pay back before we started buying $140,000 cars.

I called a meeting and suggested my business partner show us the accounts after a few late payments on rent even though we'd all paid him on time. He arrived at the meeting in the new M3. Our jaws dropped. He'd bought it. How stupid could he be?! It was at that moment that I decided he was a liability.

I was leaving the office one day when I discovered that he had paid nothing towards that month's rent and we owed almost $14,000, despite each of us giving him cash for our quarter share. I went into his office, looked through his stuff, and found a bunch of needles in his top drawer. Was he shooting up? No way. *Yes* way. He was an addict. We didn't even know it, but the money we gave him was going towards three things: a Meth habit, a car he couldn't afford, and a gambling problem he and his friend had. I was pissed! I called a meeting again, and he never showed. Avoiding us all like the plague, he knew something was up, so he never returned to the office. He left us with a huge mess to clean up.

Catastrophe had struck again. I still didn't cry.

A Multi-Million Dollar Idea

In 2016 I had an idea to turn the Holden factory into the world's largest medical cannabis facility after reading about the industry online. By this point I was drowning in debt courtesy of my ex-business partner, leases that hadn't been paid, and now electrical companies were chasing me for money because all building responsibility had been passed to me. At the same time, with all this hanging over my head, I needed to convince the state government to legalise medical cannabis because I saw a huge opportunity to create jobs and money for the state.

I pitched it to Shane. Shane set out to bring in capital from the US to build a huge medical cannabis facility at Holden's, the old car manufacturing factory. We started a new company, ACC. We brought in Ben to set up deals with companies in the US, and had the government at the table to work with us. I honestly thought all of my problems would be solved with the amount of money we were set to make.

We had a deal with the local research institute which was worth circa $40 million for the company, and investors lining up out the door. Until, that is, Shane thought it would be a good idea to get into an argument with the state premier at a function. The media wanted to know why South Australia's newest Adelaide company was fighting with the government. We said nothing and promised not to say anything.

Shane got drunk (as he did daily) and figured it would be a good idea to send our private and confidential document to the media about our deal with the research institute. They printed the success story. Bad move.

We received the signed document on Thursday, and celebrated that night. It was a good time, and everyone was in our corner. We were on a path to success. IPO (Initial Public Offering) was in sight, and I was convinced we would be a $100m company by year-end.

Things cooled off, and we were working hard. The government gave us 90 days to give us a clear path for legal changes and publicly had a roundtable meeting with other local cannabis companies. 91 days passed. Shane got drunk and posted about his fight with the premier on social media. It opened the biggest can of worms. It was all over the news for days, and before we knew it, the research institute pulled our contract for collaboration. Goodbye IPO. Goodbye to investor capital. And goodbye $40m contract.

Ben and I were fuming. We knew we needed to get out of the relationship as Shane was a loose cannon. We did and ended up spending $30,000 in legal costs keeping Shane from trying to sue us. He was such a child about it. He posted Ben's resignation letter to Facebook, and that was all in the media too. I couldn't go anywhere. Shane and I had fallen out, and I was losing faith in all people around me. Shane turned out to be a master manipulator, and everyone came out of the woodwork to tell us how bad of a person he was.

Ben called me and said it was over. There was no path forward. Still, I didn't cry.

Boys Do Cry

We took a break and tried to work out what to do next. We kicked off negotiations again and worked to rebuild the relationships we'd lost because of Shane. Before we knew it, we had an offer for $7,000,000 AUD on the table. We accepted and for the first time I was confident that it was a done deal. Ben and I booked the flights to Perth to sign the deal that Friday.

On Thursday I was feeling a little sick. On Friday I woke up at 4 am on the floor of my kitchen in a ball, shaking and shivering all over. There was no way I could attend the meeting, so Ben went without me.

I should have heard from Ben by 5 pm. Silence. I called him, and he said the lunch meeting was still going. *Still going? These guys are stalling,* I thought.

Ben returned the following Monday with bad news. The deal was off.

'I don't like these guys,' he said. And just like that, the opportunity of $7,000,000 was off the table.

By this time I was working part-time in finance to pay the bills, and was planning on taking a year off to travel with my new wife. All of my plans had fallen apart again. Another huge knockback. Another dream shattered. More success taken away before my very eyes, the success that my younger self had dreamed of.

I walked into my kitchen, sat down on the floor, and finally, I cried. And I cried. And I cried. All those years of holding it all together setback after setback came flooding out. Four hours later I realised that, honestly, it's okay to cry. Boys cry too.

About the Author:

Reece Formosa is a serial entrepreneur based in Adelaide with experience in startup companies all the way up to large-scale corporations. As well as four other ventures, Reece is the co-founder of Positive Signs, bringing messages of hope and positivity through postcards, billboards, or social media to those struggling in their everyday lives.

Connect with Reece:

Website: www.positivesigns.net.au

Taking the Leap
By Eugene Stuchinsky

'Life is like a box of chocolates. You never know what you're gonna get' ~ Forrest Gump

I was six before I had to go to school. I was wearing glasses, so everybody made fun of me. Besides that, I was very short. Everybody pushed me around. There were times when I felt like crying. There were times when I wasn't happy about it, but you know what? Being a Leo, I guess it's born in you that you have to be tough. You have to go through it.

Between the ages of 11 to 14, I got taller and went from being 5'3' to 5'9' in a matter of two years. All those kids who had been abusing me during first, second, third, fourth, fifth grade, etc. felt the payback for everything that had happened to me during those younger years in my life.

They started walking on the other side of the street when they would see me coming towards them. Most of them stayed far away from me. I have always been a very laid-back person. I was very patient with all those kids, but when the time came, they all felt it.

Do Your Best

I was always told to do my best. 'It's going to pay off in the long run. Graduate from high school, go to college, find a typical 9 to 5 job, work there for 20 years, and get a pension one day.'

Even though I didn't agree, I did it all. I graduated from high school and graduated from college with a Bachelor's degree. My first salary was a mere 24,000 dollars a year.

One day, I thought: *Man, my college loan is $40K and my yearly salary is only $24K. How is that even possible? Why did I bother going through four years of hard schooling? What is this degree worth anyways?*

I started digging and digging. Ten years later I decided that the rat race was not my thing. I discovered quite a bit about myself in those days including the fact that I cannot have a boss. I get irritated when I'm bossed around. When people come and start talking to me like that, I refuse to deal with them.

I spoke with one of my mentors about it. He was a retired CEO, and he said, 'Look, you have enough talent to make it on your own. You don't need anybody else. Just go out there, find what you're good at, find your passion, and put yourself out there.'

My first job out of college was with an international import and export company. I was working with this little, sweet lady from South America. She didn't speak perfect English, and she was so nice. She had probably been working with this company for 20 years. One day she said to me, 'You know what? I think you're going to be successful someday.'

I said, 'Why do you say this?'

'Something about you tells me you'll be successful. You'll just have to take my words and believe in them. Everybody who I have said will do well... it actually happened to them,' she said.

When the economy crashed, I was working for one of the biggest manufacturing companies in the United States. When they decided to downsize, I was one of the first people to get laid off since I held the second highest paid position there.

While I was searching, a billion-dollar international transportation company approached me saying, 'You know what Eugene? You've been through college; you know your stuff, why don't you start working with us? Here's the big yellow book (the national phone directory), start dialling. You don't work for us. We'll be co-partners. We'll give you tools, we'll pay your bills, but you have to run as your own company.'

The first week, I called one hundred people a day. On the phone, every day, a hundred people, from 7:00 am to 7:00 pm. For the first few days, I was getting *no, no, no. We're not interested. No, no, no.* By the fifth day, I got my first customer. By the tenth day, I got my tenth customer. And that's how it all started. From that point on, it was just like ice skating. It opened everything up.

People started telling other people. The customers started talking between each other, and in one year I had the highest branch in the entire company. Over a million dollars in sales.

Growing Up

I grew up in a city that had a big nuclear power station. It was one of the biggest nuclear power stations in the Ukraine. My father was an engineer there. When I was 8, my parents and I moved about 9 hours by train from that area after my father got promoted.

My grandparents didn't move with us. They lived in the

same city where I was born. At age 10, my grandfather passed away. At age 13, my uncle left for another country from the town where my grandmother was. My mom decided this was a good time for me to go and live with my grandmother, to help her out and keep her company. This way she wouldn't be alone. Even though my grandma was a fairly young grandma at that time, she was in her early 60's; my mom didn't like the thought of her being all alone.

I always liked to go to Grandma's. I had my original friends there, including some really close friends. We would hang out together every summer. So, I figured, *hey, no parents. Just me and my grandma. I can do whatever I want to do, in my own time, and hang out with all my friends. How bad could it be?*

It actually was better for me than staying at home and babysitting my little brother who at that point was four years old. This way I figured I could get away from his nagging. We also knew we were planning to go to America as soon as our paperwork was complete. My grandma's brother left before we did. Three years later my immediate family and grandma did the same once our refugee status was approved. My grandmother's brother, my great uncle, arrived in the US ahead of us.

Our first two years in the US were the most miserable years of my life. At age 15, they threw me into high school.

Despite being nearly 16, they said, 'We cannot put you in as a senior because you don't speak English.' So, I lost two years before I could graduate. Not a great experience for the Leo lion personality.

For those first two years, I felt like I was blind and deaf. As if I couldn't hear or see *anything*. Once again, the kids were making fun of me.

But the advantage to me was that my mom didn't speak English back then either. My teachers would call and say something negative about me, and she'd say, 'Okay, he's doing good? Okay, fine!' And she would hang up the phone. I never got in trouble, like really, really in trouble. It was nothing crazy.

So, how did I learn English? This is another story. I got a job in a shoe store. Two Polish girls who worked there with me would correct me every time I would say something wrong (Polish is pretty similar to my language). If I didn't know the words to say or if I couldn't remember, they would fill me in or help me out with an answer.

That's how I started learning English, little by little, talking to different people like the grandmothers who would come into the shoe store and complain about their children and/or grandchildren.

Finding Love

I met a few girls before meeting my wife Irina online. She was always finding excuses for not meeting face-to-face. I was talking to her for over two years before she decided to meet me.

Being a Leo, my emotions are very hard to get to or even read. I would probably say by the 4th or 5th date I knew I wanted to marry her. I met her parents. She met my parents. So, things started moving along. About a year later, she said, 'Why don't we move in together?' And I said, 'Okay, deal!'

We decided to move in together and live together for a year to see what it would bring us. If we could maintain our relationship and grow our love while living under the same roof, then we would move forward. If not, we would go our separate ways.

I proposed to her the second year we were together, and we were married a year later. Back then, the thinking was, *we're too young to have kids*. Irina was getting her Master's degree. We both knew that if kids entered the picture too soon, she would never get around to finishing school.

Little did we know how long we would be waiting once we

decided it was time to start a family. It took us about five years until we finally got our identical twin girls. We also had no clue that they would be born early.

Sadness and Joy

The first time I really cried in my life was when my grandpa passed away. That was a really hard time for me. The second time was when my uncle, who had immigrated with his family to another country, suddenly passed away at age 42. And then the third time was when my babies were born. That was more like the cry of joy.

Isabella went home with Irina and Brianna had to stay longer at the hospital. Irina dealt with postpartum depression and felt very guilty for not being able to visit Brianna more than a few times while she was hospitalised in the intensive care unit. I was there pretty much every day, and Irina was there maybe twice in the whole three weeks because she just couldn't visit. For her it was such a depressing thing to see our little baby laying in the crib with the tubes pumping, knowing that this baby who weighed a little over four pounds couldn't even hold a normal temperature, and she couldn't do anything for her.

Irina did the crying for both of us, while I seemed to hold it together.

Every time I would go to the hospital and see Brianna there, it was like torture. I would cry after I left. I never cried in the hospital. I would go out to my car and cry a little bit. I would head home and have to be normal again before I walked in the door. I didn't want Irina to see me all upset, so I'd walk in with a smile on my face.

The funniest thing was that every time I came to the hospital and offered my daughter my finger, she would grab it as hard as she could. Like she knew who I was. The doctor said, 'It would be very helpful if you brought her twin sister's blanket with you the next time you visit.' I did, and it helped.

Brianna started gaining momentum and was holding her temperature. She was eating better as well. She was growing a little bit, pound-by-pound-by-pound. And then finally, two weeks later, the doctors said, 'You know what? We're going to do the test for her to see if she's able to sit in a car seat. This way, you can bring her home. We'll discharge her. She's okay in the crib, now.'

She failed that test three times. Every day, I would call and say, 'Is she ready to go home?'

'Nope, not yet. She failed the test last night.'

'Can she go home?'

'Nope, not yet. She failed the test again.'

After Brianna got home, everything went pretty much back to normal. The girls started holding hands. Brianna started gaining weight quicker than her sister did, and then at one point, they were pretty much equal. Nobody could see the difference, and who was who. Even to me, in the beginning, they were so identical. We had to keep the bracelet on their feet to make sure that we fed the right baby.

Life is Good

When I'm not worried about tomorrow, life is good. Waking up in the morning, I know I have food, I have shelter, I know I can go on vacation. I know I have plenty of what I need to support our needs on a daily basis. And I think that's part of 'Life is good'.

When I feel great, it's an exciting moment. When my kids get home from school, I go with them to their activities. They love competitive dance and karate. My wife is a licensed psychotherapist and integrative nutrition health coach. She also works a full-time job outside of our home as a healthcare administrator. So, when she gets home around dinner time, I enjoy that moment as well.

There are days when I don't want to wake up in the morning. I do have days where I think: *Oh, I wish I worked for somebody else so I could count on a paycheck at the end of the week and not always have to be thinking outside the box. Life is hard. How am I going to pay my next bill? Maybe what I have right now is not for me.* Ego talks to me every day. 'You should get a corporate job. Get a $100K salary every year. Work 9 to 5 so you can leave at the end of the day, go home, relax, and be happy.'

But it's never going to happen. I'm not going to go that route again and be miserable like I was for those 15 years I spent in the rat race. I don't want to see miserable people around me. I've always been attracted to only positive people in my life. I guess I feel that if I'm going to be miserable, I'm going to attract miserable people to me. I would say that I did my best to get rid of all that emotional baggage.

About the Author:

Eugene Stuchinsky almost died at age two from a high fever. Born with an inverted club foot and a lazy eye, Eugene is no stranger to pain and surgery. He is now an official bionic man after receiving an artificial ankle at age 38. Family is very important to him. Eugene took care of his grandmother when he was only 13 years old. As a father, he took care of his identical preemie twin girls while making a million dollars in the first year of going into business for himself.

Connect with Eugene:

Email: eugenestuch@gmail.com

Printed in Poland
by Amazon Fulfillment
Poland Sp. z o.o., Wrocław